The
Parentalk
Guide to the
Childhood
Years

Also by Steve Chalke

How to Succeed as a Parent
More than Meets the Eye
The Parentalk Guide to the Teenage Years
Sex Matters

The **Paren**talk Guide to the Childhood Years

Steve Chalke

Hodder & Stoughton

LONDON SYDNEY AUCKLAND

Copyright © 1999 by Steve Chalke

First published in Great Britain in 1999

The right of Steve Chalke to be identified as the Author of
the Work has been asserted by him in accordance with the
Copyright, Designs and Patents Act 1988.

10 9 8 7 6 5 4 3 2 1

British Library Cataloguing in Publication Data
A record for this book is available from the British Library

ISBN 0 340 72168 5

Typeset in Monotype Sabon by
Strathmore Publishing Services, London N7

Printed and bound in Great Britain by
Clays Ltd, St Ives PLC

Hodder and Stoughton Ltd
A division of Hodder Headline PLC
338 Euston Road
London NW1 3BH

CONTENTS

Part Three: Friends

FOREWORD

When I look back on my childhood it seems it was always sunny. Everything feels surrounded by a golden haze. Those trips to the seaside with my mum and dad; playing outside on long, hot summer nights for hours on end; pretending to be Batgirl by turning my duffel coat into a magic cape; and my mum reading me bedtime stories. I was a very lucky girl who had parents who seemed somehow to know instinctively what to do.

I'm sure, however, that they were just as scared and baffled by the responsibility of parenthood as I was when my Rosie was born. I want her to have a happy, safe, glorious childhood, cocooned in love, warmth and security. But how do we know we are getting it right?

That's where this book can help and why it is such a tonic. It reminds you that you are doing a good job. It reassures you in areas you might be struggling with and offers some very helpful and positive suggestions on how to make things even better. Babies don't come out of the womb clutching a set of instructions in their tiny little hands: but this book will certainly go a long way to helping you get the best out of the most rewarding job in the world – being a parent!

I hope it will help you too …

Lorraine Kelly
LONDON, *October 1998*

INTRODUCTION

Being a parent is, at one and the same time, the most wonderful privilege and the most daunting challenge of your life. This 'small task' will stretch you more than anything you've attempted before … and probably more than anything you'll ever face in the future. But for those who're willing to put in the effort, it can also be the most exciting, rewarding and fulfilling experience of your life!

If you're anything like me, there's a nagging feeling at the back of your mind that everyone else is doing a better job of being a parent than you are. But the truth is, they're not. We all make mistakes. None of us is perfect. We all do and say things that, with hindsight, we wish we hadn't.

In over fifteen years of dealing with family problems – both personally and professionally – I've come across very few parents who have any real confidence in their ability to do a good job. Though most mums and dads actually do an *excellent* job, they fall into the trap of measuring their performance against totally unrealistic 'ideals', and then feel inadequate when they can't match up.

The fact of the matter is, you'll never be a *perfect* parent. But not only can you be a good parent, you can even be a *great* parent – one your child is really proud of. And to achieve it, all you need are the three essential qualities available to every mum or dad whatever their situation in life: love, time and a little bit of self-trust.

Families aren't standard issue. They come in all shapes and sizes – not just the classic Hollywood version of mum, dad, two kids and a dog. There are models with one child and those with six – even those where all six were born together! There are those where the children, or some of them, have been adopted, and those where one is physically disabled or has a learning disability. And, for all sorts of reasons, there are those with just one parent – sometimes a mum, sometimes a dad. Sometimes there's a step-parent and step-children. But whatever your family looks like, this book is for you.

There are, of course, many reasons why you might be reading it: you may simply be looking for reassurance that what you're doing as a mum or dad is along the right lines; or you may need urgent help. Perhaps your child is in some kind of trouble, and you want to know what to do about it.

This book is about the basic principles and skills that every parent, regardless of their individual circumstances, needs in order not only to *survive* being a parent, but to *thrive*. But be warned: they're *not* short-cuts. They all require effort. The reason for this is simple: short-cuts just don't work.

So read on, because the relationship that any child has with their parent is the most formative and influential one of their lives. That's why my hope and sincere prayer is that this book serves you well.

PART ONE: HOME

The Measure of a Man

How Can I Give My Child Self-Worth?

Jeremy had it all: a good job, a fancy wardrobe, plenty of money, lots of good friends, a high class education, a chauffeur-driven limousine, and an open door to the best social events. He was universally popular both personally and at work, where he was tipped for the top job in the company when the chief executive retired in a few years' time.

Then, one day, it all went wrong. Nervous dealing on the Tokyo stock exchange sent the company's share price plummetting. As a result, a major customer lost confidence in the firm, and a deal that would have secured everyone's future for the next ten years fell through. Jeremy got the blame – and the sack! What's more, having invested most of his savings in company shares that were now almost worthless, he had no money. Upset, and unsure what to do, he turned to his friends for help. After all, as the saying goes, 'a friend in need is a friend indeed'. But they couldn't drop him fast enough, discarding him as soon as his usefulness to them had come to an end.

The truth is that, throughout their life, your child, just like you, will be accepted or rejected on the basis of how they perform or what they have to offer. Most people we meet in life have time for us, or not, because of our looks, skills, connections or money – in short, because we can offer them something they need or want. It's not pleasant and it's a hard lesson to learn, but it's the way the world is: most people are only interested in us when we're 'successful'.

But as a mum or dad, it's *your* job to be the big exception to this rule. You've got to love your child, not for what they can offer, but for who they are – with no strings attached – and to make sure they know it.

 Top Tip: Every parent's primary task is to love their child unconditionally and prove it.

The Man in the White Suit

Tony's job takes him around the world. On one occasion, he found himself sitting on a plane across the aisle from a ten-year-old girl who was obviously returning to her family after a term away at boarding school. At first he was surprised she was flying alone in business class. But he slowly became fascinated by the fact that she was eating and drinking absolutely everything that was put in front of her, and then summoning the flight attendants for more.

Ignoring the work he was meant to be doing, he watched her closely from behind his newspaper. She was clearly making the most of her first unaccompanied flight. But as a seasoned flyer, Tony knew how unwise it was to eat so much. Sooner or later, what goes down in such large quantities often comes back up again! Sure enough, by the time the plane touched down she was looking decidedly green. And as she walked down the gangway, she threw up all over her dress.

Following her down the steps, Tony could see a man in an immaculately pressed white suit running across the tarmac, waving at her. From the expression on his face, Tony guessed this was the girl's dad. But any doubt lingering in his mind was dispelled when, despite the state of her dress, he threw his arms around her without a moment's hesitation, enfolding her in a massive hug. As they turned and began to walk back to the terminal together, his expensive and once elegant suit now permanently stained with vomit, all Tony could see in the man's eyes was joy at being with his daughter again. That's unconditional love.

We all need this kind of unconditional, no-strings-attached love to be happy. If we never receive it, we end up heading through life constantly trying to please people in order to *make* them love us, crippled by the fear that we'll accidentally do something to make them stop loving us. But on top of that, if we've never experienced unconditional love and acceptance, it's all too easy to get our three basic human needs – love, security and significance – confused with sex, money and power – which always has disastrous consequences.

What's more, according to recent research, children who don't feel loved by their parents are more likely to be sexually promiscuous as teenagers than those whose homes are secure and loving. In other words, if your kids aren't sure you love them unconditionally, they may well go looking for love elsewhere – quite possibly in all the wrong places – and sometimes greatly to their cost.

Top Tip: *Your child needs your unconditional love to survive and thrive in life.*

The Right Stuff

Being a parent is a wonderful experience, but it's also a huge responsibility. What we do today has a fundamental impact on what our children become tomorrow. The main responsibility for producing mature, self-disciplined, well motivated and balanced adult members of society belongs not to the school, the scouts, the government, the media or wider society – though all these undoubtedly help or hinder – but to parents. And unconditional love is the greatest gift any parent can ever give their child, because it's the prime ingredient in building a firm foundation for the whole of their life.

One of the things Cornelia and I most liked about our first house when we moved in was the garden patio, which the previous owners had laid in order to enjoy the afternoon sun. However, after a couple of years we noticed that some of the patio slabs were starting to sink a bit, whilst others were becoming uneven. Eventually, it got so bad – and so dangerous for our two young toddlers – that we realised we'd have to take the slabs up and level the ground again. But when a couple of friends and I removed all the slabs, we discovered why the patio had slowly been subsiding: rather than laying down a proper foundation of rubble and gravel, and then a layer of sand, the previous owners had simply flattened the earth and plonked the slabs down on top.

Foundations are vital. Without them, you're in massive trouble. And childhood is the foundation for the rest of life. Whatever we build on top in later life will only survive if the foundation is deep enough and strong enough to support it. A friend of mine, remembering his own sometimes difficult childhood, often tells me that his aim is to give his kids the loving, stable family environment he never had. He wants them to know just how much he loves them, but he's not always convinced he's doing too well. When he's in a confident mood, he imagines his children will graduate from university with first class degrees and walk into top jobs in the City, taking out full-colour adverts in all the major newspapers thanking him for making them the happiest, most confident, most well-adjusted people in the world. But on the days when everything seems to be going wrong, he imagines them becoming human sponges, totally reliant on their friends and completely incapable of holding down a job or a long-term relationship. And it's *his* fault because he didn't get it right. He didn't manage to inject into them the self-esteem they needed to be happy, stable and confident.

The funny thing is, unconditional love is the one gift that *every* parent can afford to give their child. It doesn't matter how rich or poor you are – we're all on a level playing field and no one has a head start on anyone else. Money and presents are no substitute for unconditional love. But by clearly and persistently showing your children that you'll always love them, no matter what they do, you can grant them the self-confidence, security and self-esteem they'll need to be happy throughout life's journey.

Top Tip: Build a firm foundation for your child's future happiness – let them know how much you love them today.

Act Naturally

My friend Philippa has identical twin boys. Most people, including me, have huge trouble telling them apart. But right from the moment they were born, Philippa says that she has never had any difficulty knowing which is which. They may be 'genotypically' identical – meaning that every strand and sequence of their DNA is precisely the same – but their behaviour, tastes and personalities are quite distinct from one another. And because the rest of the world labels them as 'identical', she encourages them to explore their differences at every opportunity. 'I want them to know that, even though they look exactly the same and people sometimes treat them as if they were interchangeable, they're actually entirely unique. There's no one else quite like either of them, which makes each of them special and uniquely valuable.'

This is exactly the message our children need to hear from us. Without making them arrogant, our task is to ensure they know that the world is a better place for having them in it. If life is a journey, *unconditional* love – loving your child with no strings attached – supplies them with the strength and inner resources not only to see it through, but to enjoy travelling. By showing your kids that you love them unconditionally, you're proving to them that they're intrinsically valuable and individually unique human beings, quite apart from their performance or whatever assets they may have.

Of course, loving their children unconditionally isn't hard for most parents. It comes naturally. When Sam was arrested for joyriding with a friend, his mum was asked to accompany him to the police station. Only twelve years old, he was easily led, so this wasn't the first brush he'd had with the law. Sam's mum was clearly at the end of her tether as they waited for the solicitor to arrive. But as the police officer who carried out the interview later commented, in spite of her anger with her son, there was no escaping her obvious love for him. She couldn't hide it. However badly he behaved, however disobedient he was and whatever trouble he got himself into, she just couldn't help loving him. She loved him because she loved him, and for no other reason. That's unconditional love.

There's an instant, natural, biological bond of love between mums and their kids. And even for dads, who haven't carried the child for nine months, there's a kind of irresistible magnetism. A baby's big eyes, little face, gawky behaviour and vulnerability all draw out our parental instincts. In fact, some scientists say that babies deliberately evolved to look like this in order to trigger our parental and loving instincts, and to get us oohing and aahing.

The feeling isn't entirely one-sided, of course. Children grow up instinctively loving and trusting their parents. They want and need our attention and acceptance. But though they'll take it for granted that we love them when they're toddlers, our kids naturally start to question their previous assumptions as they get older – including our unreserved and unconditional love for them. That's why it's so important to work hard at providing them with ongoing absolute proof positive that we love them, and that we'll always love them, not matter what they do.

Top Tip: *Your child is never too old to hear that you love them, so never stop telling them.*

Great Expectations

But even if we regularly tell our kids we love them with no strings attached, it's no good if everything else we say and do sends them a different message. We all want our kids to do well, for instance, so they can live happy and successful lives. And we know that this means giving them a push to succeed, both at school and elsewhere. But tragically, the way in which many parents do this is almost guaranteed to backfire.

If our children believe, or even suspect, that we love them more when they succeed than when they fail, they'll naturally try to succeed in order to win our approval. But in the process, they'll stop believing we love them unconditionally and start to link love with achievement. And when that happens, in pushing our children to make the best of their lives – something we only do 'for their own good' – we'll ironically have ended up failing them as parents.

A few years ago, a friend of mine received a letter that he never forgot. 'Dear Dave,' it said, 'I was so touched by what you said on the radio the other day. You see, I don't really like myself very much. All my life I've felt like a failure. I've never felt able to match up to my parents' expectations of me. However hard I've tried, I've never been good enough. It's just so hard to talk about it, though I know I need to. Yours sincerely, Mary.' It was a sad letter, though not the only one like it that Dave had received after a radio interview in which he'd spoken publicly about his own relationship with his parents. But what etched this particular letter firmly into his mind was the postscript, hastily scrawled at the bottom of the page: 'PS. I'm eighty-one.'

Of course, it's natural to have high hopes, expectations and standards for your child. In fact, if we didn't push them at all, they'd begin to wonder if we *cared* how they turned out. A bit of pressure and challenge is good for them. But it's a delicate balance, because *too much* pressure is crippling. Rather than being constructive, it becomes destructive.

Jill always used to hate the incentive prizes her father dangled in front of her to do well at school. She knew he only offered them out of a real desire to see her do the best she could, but she couldn't help feeling that they somehow proved he loved her more when she did well than he did when she didn't. 'I know he didn't mean to,' she says, 'but by using incentives he sent me a very mixed message.

On the one hand he was always saying that he loved me, pass or fail. But on the other, it was like I was failing him personally if I didn't pass – and the resulting absence of any prize was the proof. I never felt he was really proud of me. I knew he was disappointed when I failed, and not getting the prize just rubbed it in. But what hurt most was the feeling that whenever he withheld a present, he was withholding his love as well.'

 Top Tip: *Never link your love with your child's achievement – it's a recipe for disaster.*

Slightly Used Cocoon, One Careful Owner

If your child's self-esteem is pinned to success, and measured in those terms, they're doomed to live their whole life with a sense of failure and guilt. Why? Because life is competitive. Like it or not, that's just the way it is. From school tests to job interviews, we're surrounded by competition all of the time – there's absolutely nothing we can do to change that. And because life is competitive, there are always going to be winners and losers. There's nothing we can do to change that, either.

My children's school, like many others, has a 'house points' system as a way of rewarding outstanding work or behaviour. If you get fifty house points in a term – no small achievement – you're entitled to sign the book. The third time you sign the book, you become eligible to wear a special tie with the school uniform.

During the whole of her time at the school, our elder daughter, Emily, signed the book twice. Our elder son, Daniel, now doing his GCSEs, has also signed the book twice. But Abigail, our third child, had signed the book three times and qualified for the tie before the end of her first year!

Seeing your achievements eclipsed by someone else is always hard – especially when it's your little sister. In fact, some schools in the past have deliberately avoided having competitive systems such as house points precisely so they can spare those pupils who wouldn't do so well the heartache of 'failure'. But the problem is that this misguided approach can, at best, only prolong the inevitable onset of competition. It can't remove it altogether. And besides, even without the house points system, Emily and Daniel would soon have realised that Abigail was doing better than they had at her age – at least as far as those things for which you can get house points are concerned.

Sooner or later, every child has to deal with competition. You can't hide them away for ever, safe in their own little cocoon, because one day, sooner than you think, they'll inevitably turn into a butterfly and fly off to face the real world. If you don't prepare them for that moment, who will? Part of every responsible parent's job is to help their children cope with competition, rather than pretending the world isn't really like that.

 Top Tip: *Don't protect your child from competition: prepare them for it.*

The Good, the Bad and the Ugly

But desperately trying to groom your child for success, hoping if they're good enough they'll never have to deal with disappointment, is just as short-sighted. One of the biggest problems with expecting your child to succeed all the time is, of course, that no one actually does. Even gifted children fail sooner or later. It's as inevitable as competition. Whoever you are, you can't win everything. Your child, like you, will spend their whole life meeting people who're faster, cleverer, richer, more attractive and more inventive than they are. And it won't matter how good a tennis player, footballer, artist, musician, writer, speaker, actor, entrepreneur, racing driver or accountant they are, there'll always be someone faster, better or younger waiting to take their place.

Eric Liddell – hero of the film *Chariots of Fire* – was no stranger to breaking records. During his career as a runner, he'd seen one record after another tumble to his astonishing speed. Favourite to win the 100 yards gold medal at the 1924 Paris Oympic Games, he shocked and amazed the public by refusing to take part in the heats because they fell on a Sunday. He knew he'd be disqualified from the final, and that his rival, Harold Abrahams, would probably take both the medal and the record, but some things were more important to him than winning, and his religious convictions wouldn't let him run on a Sunday. Instead, he won the 400 yards – a distance he'd never run competitively before – by a full five yards, smashing the existing record with a time of 47.6 seconds.

But after achieving one of the greatest victories in Olympic history, Liddell chose to retire from competitive running and return to the city in China where he was born, to become a teacher. He knew that for a runner the only way to go, after winning Olympic Gold, was down, and that sooner or later someone younger and fitter would break his records just as he'd broken those of the runners before him. He also knew that there was more to life than winning and that, in the words of the Olympic motto, what mattered in the long run was 'not the winning, but the taking part'.

What's more, in the famous words of John Donne, 'No man is an island'. There isn't much in life that we do entirely on our own. Most of life is about being part of a team, whether at home, school, work, or anywhere else. And since a team, like a chain, is only as strong as its weakest link, you can guarantee that sooner or later your child is going to be disappointed as a result of *someone's* performance, even if it isn't their own! So it's vital that you teach your son or daughter how to cope with disappointment and failure now, rather than postponing the lesson until later. Because if you teach your child how to succeed, but not how to cope with failure or just plain ordinariness, you're not actually doing them any long-term favours.

 Top Tip: *Failure is inevitable, so teach your child to cope with it by letting them know you love them unconditionally.*

'I Have a Dream …'

Some parents worry that if they prepare their child for disappointment, they run the risk of actually setting them up to fail. After all, if you teach your kids that it doesn't matter if they fail or succeed, what incentive are you giving them to succeed? If you don't keep the pressure up, won't that just encourage them not to put in the effort, settling for mediocre results when they're capable of so much more?

But the truth is that children play better, learn better, concentrate better, relate better, laugh more, give more and love more when they feel unconditionally loved than when they don't. This doesn't mean they'll be straight-A students or Olympic athletes. It's just that if they know you love them whatever, they'll be happy and content with themselves. If your child knows they're loved in this way, it will act as a kind of internal compass to help steer them through all life's inevitable knocks and disappointments. Martin Luther King called love 'the most durable power' in the world, giving people the strength to overcome the greatest odds to achieve their ultimate goal.

On a trip to the Far East a few years ago, I visited a wonderful project called Rainbow House. In the surrounding countryside, hundreds of children are completely abandoned by their parents because they have disabilities ranging from severe mental or physical handicap to something as minor as a cleft palate. Government homes – under-resourced and overstretched – are left to be responsible for them. Tragically, they can rarely do any more than provide food, shelter and basic medical care. The children, starved of attention, stimulation and love, are simply left to vegetate, often three or four to a bed.

But in the middle of this terrible human misery, Rainbow House is a beacon of hope. Through the dedicated work of its staff, it's able to negotiate with the authorities and offer a new start to some of the children. I was introduced to one six-year-old girl who had recently been rescued. Her only 'crime' was to have been born with a harelip. She was intelligent, warm, kind and full of life. But the staff told me that a year ago, when she had first been brought in, she had been incontinent and couldn't even speak. In fact, without their intervention, she would almost certainly have died. But because of all the love, care and security thay had showered on her, she was growing into the happy, self-confident child she'd always had the potential to be.

We want our children to do well, but doing well doesn't always mean being 'perfect'. It means using your abilities to their full potential and making the most of what you've got. And the key to unlocking this potential is a parent's unconditional love. If we want our kids to do well, we need to ensure they know that we love them whether they win or lose.

Top Tip: *Knowing you love them unconditionally is the best motivation you can give your child to do well.*

The Power of Positive Thinking

So how *does* a parent motivate their child to fulfil their potential, at the same time as ensuring they know they're loved unconditionally? Well, like adults, children do well when they feel confident about themselves. They feel confident about themselves when they know they're doing well. And know they're doing well when they're *told* they're doing well. There's a natural and automatic connection.

We all understand the power of a negative mental 'association'. That's why we punish our kids for doing something bad. We rely on them associating the punishment with the 'crime' and hope it'll make them think twice next time. But positive associations are just as important. Your child *wants* to feel valued and appreciated, so if you praise them when they do something right, they'll be more likely to do it again. And if you praise them for their effort, they'll want to try just as hard, if not harder, in the future.

When his young daughter brought him breakfast in bed one Saturday morning, Frank, always cynical, suspected she might have been put up to the idea rather than coming up with it on her own. Nevertheless, delighted at being pampered in such a way and never one to look a gift horse in the mouth, he praised his daughter wholeheartedly for being so 'caring, considerate and spontaneous'. He could tell she enjoyed the praise, but was surprised when, the next Saturday, she arrived in the bedroom once more with breakfast in bed. Again he thanked her and again she brought him breakfast in bed the next Satruday. In fact, it became a regular thing, and she only stopped when, having put on a stone in weight in a few short months, Frank decided that his waistband couldn't take too much of a good thing and specifically asked her not to bring him breakfast in bed any more!

Just as a flower blooms when you give it enough water, and dies when you neglect it, so your child's self-image will bloom when you praise them and wither when you don't. Experts call this the Law of

Reinforcement – 'behaviour with desirable consequences will recur' – but to most of us it just seems like plain, old-fashioned common sense.

 Top Tip: *Catch your child red-handed doing something right – and praise them for it!*

The Seven Steps to Happiness

As you praise your child, be careful to steer clear of the following common pitfalls:

1 **Avoid fake praise.** Never allow your desire to praise your child to push you into lying to them. Insincere praise won't help them. It's patronising, and has the effect of completely devaluing any genuine praise you offer them on other occasions.

2 **Avoid vague praise.** Always be specific. That way, your child will know *exactly* what they did right, and will learn to recognise their strengths. Don't just say, 'That was good.' Explain why it was good.

3 **Avoid achievement-related praise.** If you praise your child only for their achievements, they'll begin to link your approval and love with their success. As a result, the self-esteem you're trying to establish will be destroyed. So praise them for their effort, choices, thoughtfulness, independence, skills, helpfulness or ideas, *not* only their success.

4 **Avoid qualified praise.** If you follow your praise with a lecture

19

on how your child could have done *even better* if only they'd done this or that, you'll send the message that their effort wasn't quite good enough. They'll remember the criticism but not the praise. (Experts reckon it takes eighteen pieces of praise to counteract the effects of just one piece of negative criticism!)

5   **Avoid comparative praise.** Never say, 'You were better than so and so'. And above all, don't praise them for being 'the best'. It's doing *their* best that counts. Help your child measure their effort against *their* standards, not someone else's.

6   **Avoid manipulative praise.** Never praise people to 'warm them up' for a favour. 'That's great, love ... Now get us a cup of tea, will you?' Even if your praise is real, by linking it to a request it'll seem insincere.

7   **Avoid material praise.** Don't give incentives: 'If you do well in your exams, I'll get you that bike you wanted.' If they fail, you'll have to withhold a present just when your child needs to feel your love and acceptance the most. And the situation's not much better if they succeed. If you want to give your child a gift, give it, being careful not to spoil them. But never use treats as incentives.

 Top Tip: *Praise lets your child identify what they're good at, which helps them see their unique value.*

'Spare the Rod, Spoil the Child?'

How Should I Discipline My Child?

One South African game reserve has a big problem. Experts there are worried about some of their young male elephants, who're behaving very badly. They're attacking tourists and trying to mate with female white rhinos. In fact, over three years, nineteen rhinos have been gored to death and one rogue elephant even killed the professional hunter who was sent in to shoot it. Experts are unanimous: the young elephants' unusually aggressive and violent behaviour is the result of never having been disciplined and nurtured by a 'matriarchal female'. Put simply, they're missing their mothers!

The problem was that the young elephants were moved from one game reserve to another without their mothers or any other family members. Since they'd already been weaned, the park authorities assumed it was safe to move them. But they were wrong – and the results have been disastrous. Eddie Koch, who's looked into the problem, sums it all up: 'Like children, young elephants need discipline if they are to grow up as responsible members of society.' The young elephants 'turned delinquent because they have never been taken in hand by their elders'.

The situation is less dramatic for humans, but the same basic lesson applies: parents need to teach their child right from wrong or they'll live their lives in a destructive way, hurting others and themselves into the bargain.

Top Tip: As a parent, it's **your** job to discipline your child, teaching them right from wrong.

A Recipe for Disaster

I recently talked to a mum whose son was totally out of control. His behaviour was no longer just embarrassing: now it was dangerous. 'I just can't understand it,' she told me. 'We gave him everything he wanted.' Tragically, that *was* the problem! If a child is given everything they ask for, they come to learn they can have anything they want. And the older they get, the more problems this is bound to create.

The truth is that learning to live within limits is part of what it means to be human. So if *you* don't teach your child the difference between right and wrong – and then enforce those limits – sooner or later someone else will! And it'll hurt a lot more if that happens than if you begin to do the job now. No parent does their child any favours by allowing them to do as they please. What's more, in the end their child is bound to resent them for not preparing them adequately for life.

When Robert was born, his parents were overjoyed. They'd been trying for a baby for years, and had almost given up hope. Their only child, they spoilt him rotten. Literally. If he wanted something, they gave it to him. When he was naughty, they acted as if he'd done nothing wrong. They couldn't bear the idea of punishing him, in case he thought they didn't love him. As a result, he never knew when to stop. He misbehaved at school and became impossible to control. When the teachers told him off, he threw himself into a rage. In the playground, he regularly 'borrowed' the other kids' toys and stole their sweets whenever he felt like it. In the end, his behaviour became so bad that the school had to exclude him – first for a short time and then, when that failed, permanently.

It's an extreme example, but it shows what can happen when children aren't given a proper, creative framework of discipline. Kids always push the boundaries. It's part of growing up: learning what you can, and can't, do. But if these boundaries aren't clear and enforced, they learn that breaking them is OK.

If you don't discipline your child by teaching them the meaning of the word 'No' early on – for example, when they throw a tantrum because they want a pair of the latest hyper-expensive trainers, or another bar of chocolate or packet of crisps – then they'll assume that 'No' actually means 'Maybe', or even, if they cause enough fuss, 'Yes'. And the more boundaries they learn to ignore, the harder it becomes for them to accept any limits on their future behaviour. If you don't teach your six-year-old the meaning of the word 'No' now, don't be surprised if they become an arrogant, obnoxious and disliked sixteen-year-old. The time to defuse the teenage time bomb is ten years before it happens!

> **Top Tip:** *When you mean 'No', stick to 'No' – you're not doing your child any favours if you just let them do what they like.*

Free at Last!

It's a mistake to think of discipline as the enemy of freedom – it's actually its friend. The young South African elephants weren't given more freedom by their undisciplined upbringing. Instead, they lived in a world filled with stress, insecurity and a lack of self-discipline. If their mothers and older male elephants had been there to keep them in line, teaching them the limits of acceptable elephant behaviour, these 'juvenile delinquents' would have been able to enjoy a normal family life.

When I was ten years old, I learnt to play the piano. I wasn't very good. I hated the lessons and did everything I could to avoid practising the dreaded scales. I wanted to be able to play the piano, but I didn't like the discipline of practice. The results are obvious. My piano-playing these days is lumpy, to put it mildly. Discipline as a child in learning to play the piano wouldn't have *restricted* my freedom – it would actually have *created* it. If I'd practised properly, I'd now be able to sit down in front of our piano at home and play to my heart's content. But as it is, since they can't bear the awful racket I make whenever I try to play our piano – and who can blame them? – my family has banned me from going anywhere near it!

At ten, I thought discipline was the opposite of freedom. When my parents stopped me from doing something I wanted to do, or made me do something I didn't want to do, I thought they were taking away my freedom. Now, of course, I see how wrong I was. With the benefit of hindsight, I know that the discipline my parents instilled in me when I was younger has given me the freedom I enjoy today. The truth is that real freedom is never the *enemy* of discipline – it's the *product* of discipline.

Happy children usually come from families where love – which includes good, healthy discipline – forms the backbone of daily life. Good discipline produces respect and self-respect. And however painful it seems at the time, good discipline tells a child that you love them far too much to allow them to be destructive and self-destructive. It says, in effect, 'I love you too much to let you flush your life down the toilet!' The problem is that, as someone once complained, life has to be lived forwards, but can only be understood backwards. This, of course, is why no child (however bright) ever really understands the value of discipline until they're older.

Top Tip: Discipline doesn't **restrict** freedom, it **creates** it!

Either/Or?

Discipline has a bad press. For most of us, it's a word that conjures up Victorian images of children being 'seen but not heard'. A century ago, parents were stern, table manners were impeccable and punishment was severe. 'Spare the rod, spoil the child' was the household motto. Discipline was all about punishment, and punishment was all about the cane, the belt or – if your parents were the soft type – just the slipper!

In fact, many of us still think that 'discipline = punishment'. Nothing more, nothing less. The problem with this is that discipline and love are then seen as contradictory. You can do one or the other, but you can't love your child and discipline them in the same breath. As a result of this misunderstanding, some parents choose to underplay the role of discipline, while others steer well clear of it altogether because they see it as cruel, negative and unloving. And then, often too late, they end up wondering why they can't do anything to control their child's behaviour.

But the truth is that discipline and punishment aren't the same thing at all. Discipline is about a lot more than just punishment. In fact, punishment is only a very small part of healthy discipline, which should be overwhelmingly *positive*. And love, far from being something that contradicts discipline, is its motivation, its cause and its goal.

In 1912, the famous ship, *Titanic*, sank on its maiden voyage from Liverpool to New York. Dubbed 'unsinkable', this gigantic floating hotel plummeted to the bottom of the Atlantic Ocean with the loss of 1,500 lives after hitting an iceberg. But the interesting thing is that the iceberg did most of its damage *underneath* the water's surface, gouging a massive hole out of the side of the ship and allowing water in at an astonishing rate. In fact, it's reckoned that around 90 per cent of any iceberg is invisible, always hidden beneath the ocean waves. Only the tip – the top 10 per cent – floats above the water line.

Punishment has a part to play in good discipline. But the truth is that, though it tends to be the part that gets seen and talked about the most, it's only the tip of the iceberg. Since punishment is the most obvious form of discipline, many parents act as if that's all there is to it. So we penalise our kids for everything they do wrong, but never think (or somehow forget) to encourage them for all the things they do right. And then we wonder why they struggle to develop the self-confidence we want them to have.

There's a lot more to discipline than punishment. Praise, encouragement, thanks, listening and respect are like the other 90 per cent of the iceberg that never gets seen. They form the basis on which your child's self-esteem and self-discipline are built, and without them, all the punishment in the world will do no good, and could do a lot of harm, because your child will only know what's *wrong* with them. They won't have anything positive to build on. It's not a question of either/or: *either* punishing your child *or* praising them. Instead it's a case of both/and: in order to be effective, good discipline requires the use of *both* appropriate punishment (teaching your child when they've done something wrong) *and* praise (teaching them when they've done something right).

Discipline should be an en*abler*: a creative force designed to build maturity and consistency in your child, helping them fit into society without being swamped by it. It should be the framework and encouragement a loving parent creates to help their child gradually learn how to control their behaviour and develop self-discipline. It should give your child the self-control they need to cope, both now and in the future.

Most of the rest of this chapter is actually about punishment. But it's absolutely vital to understand that unless you constantly encourage and praise your child, none of the things you do to punish them will have the desired effect. Constant praise is the bedrock for effective punishment.

> **Top Tip:** *Discipline is about much more than punishment; without praise, none of your punishments will have the desired effect.*

'What's the Diagnosis, Doctor?'

Children misbehave in different ways and for lots of different reasons, each requiring a different course of action. That's why a parent needs to make the right diagnosis of the situation in order to make the right response.

It's critical for you not to act first and think later. Instead, do it the other way around: stop and think, very carefully, both about why your child is misbehaving and about what you're going to do about it. Take a good, hard look before you leap.

1 **Accidents.** 'Accidents *will* happen', as the saying goes. It's inevitable, so don't lay into your child for accidents – they probably feel bad enough already. For instance, if they accidentally break a window playing ball in the back garden, don't react. Think. You let them play in the garden. You probably even

28

bought them the ball. It was an 'accident waiting to happen'! (Unless, of course, you told them *not* to play ball in the garden, in which case you need to punish them for disobedience, not for breaking the window. Though it's expensive to replace, the window isn't important. But if you don't tackle their disobedience now, it'll lead to bigger trouble later on.)

2 **Mistakes.** These are short-sighted judgments or bad decisions that result from a lack of wisdom. We all make them, though with experience we hopefully make fewer and fewer. Like accidents, they're not deliberate. When one of my sons left his clarinet on the bus, it took him a full week to tell us he'd lost it. Leaving it on the bus was an accident; not telling us was a mistake. If he'd told us about it immediately, we could have phoned up the bus company and had it back the next day. He wouldn't have been punished. But because he left it a week, we decided to dock his pocket money. He had to learn to be more responsible with valuable possessions.

3 **Cries for help.** What seems like a lack of discipline can sometimes be a cry for help. If your seven-year-old misbehaves after the arrival of a new baby, is it really a cry for attention because they need to know you still love them? Is your nine-year-old's lack of interest in school actually the result of being bullied, or feeling unable to cope? It takes time to find out. Just as a doctor doesn't take one glance at a patient and simply *guess* at what the problem is, so a wise parent doesn't jump to conclusions. They're concerned enough to take time to find out *why* their child is behaving as they are.

4 **Challenges.** These are deliberate acts of rebellion. Every child

pushes limits to see where they are and, more importantly, how firmly they're fixed. When Anne took her six-year-old son to her friend Jean's house for the afternoon, she took plenty of toys for him to play with whilst she and Jean chatted. Removing them from the bag and putting them on the floor, she told him he could play with any of them he liked, but made it extremely clear that he mustn't touch Jean's prized collection of china dolls, which were displayed in a glass-fronted cabinet in the same room. 'They're not toys,' she insisted. 'Do you understand?' He nodded, sat down and started playing happily. But later, when the two women wandered into the kitchen to make a cup of tea, he leapt to his feet, opened the glass cabinet and removed one of the precious dolls. When Anne and Jean returned a few minutes later, they found him staring guiltily at the mutilated corpse of a doll that had started the day with a full set of limbs, but now lay in bits strewn across the carpet. Anne was overwhelmed with embarrassment. She apologised profusely to Jean, who assured her that it didn't matter and that the doll could easily be fixed. 'Don't blame the child,' she added. 'He was only doing what boys his age do.' But Anne knew that action had to be taken. She couldn't afford to let this deliberate act of rebellion go unanswered. She had to punish him, not just because he'd broken the doll, but more importantly because he'd deliberately disobeyed her instructions. It's as if he were throwing down the gauntlet – inviting her to a duel. If limits aren't clear and enforced, children learn that breaking them is OK. *It's absolutely vital that you meet these challenges head on and win*, or they'll come back to haunt you later, when they'll be harder to win. Maintaining your authority is a key part of winning your child's trust and respect.

 Top Tip: Make sure you find out **why** your child did what they did before you decide what kind of response to make.

Undisciplined 'Discipline'

The aim of all good discipline should be to build your child's *self-*discipline, helping them to develop as confident people who're in control of their actions, emotions and ultimately their lives. Its basic goal is to help them become architects of their future instead of its victims. But tragically, when parents are undisciplined or consistently unfair in the way they discipline their children, things fall a long way short of this.

If we're not careful, what we call 'discipline' can degenerate into nothing more than a chance for us to work off our anger or frustration with our children for their mistakes and failings. As they say, 'We all save our worst behaviour for home'. Children can't hit back, so they can become a convenient target for offloading all our frustrations at the way we've been treated by other, 'bigger' people all day long.

In fact, sometimes the 'discipline' that a parent hands out has less to do with their *child's* behaviour than with their *own*. At the end of a long day, it's easy for a parent to view their child's actions as 'the last straw'. Whether it's the noise, the mess, the questions or the demands for help, it all seems too much to cope with. So they end up lashing out, either verbally or physically. Their kids find themselves on the receiving end of their frustration, being shouted at, bawled at, grounded, banished, threatened, shaken, slapped, beaten, or even kicked or punched, for tiny violations of the rules – or worse, for no other reason than the unpredictable mood swings of their parent. It's not their fault: they just happened to be in the wrong place at the wrong time.

No punishment or discipline does any good if it's arbitrary – handed out because of the mood a parent happens to be in at the time. And no punishment is effective if it's carried out in the heat of the moment. It's easy to punish a child without really thinking it through first. But this kind of discipline is almost always undisciplined, which means that it's useless for teaching your kids any contructive lessons except to stay out of your way!

The truth is – all other arguments aside – aggressive, angry or uncontrolled lashing out doesn't actually work as a form of discipline. Its only real impact is to produce strained or broken relationships and children who may well be scarred for life. For instance, if a child is constantly spanked, the emotional shock – always more lasting than the physical pain – slowly loses its impact. And once a child is immune, the punishment is useless. As a result, parents who use these tactics get dragged into a 'vicious circle', feeling the need to resort to even more drastic measures in order to achieve the same results. But all this does is slowly turn discipline into an all-out war from which no one emerges victorious.

In fact, this kind of undisciplined 'discipline' isn't just ineffective. It's also counter-productive. Rather than building up your child's trust, respect, love, confidence and self-worth, it breaks all these things down. Rather than improving your relationship with your child, it undermines it. Eventually it'll destroy it altogether.

 Top Tip: *Undisciplined 'discipline' does more harm than good.*

A Team of Wild Horses

In the famous chariot scene from the film *Ben Hur*, Joshua Ben Hur has to race a team of powerful stallions at full speed round Rome's Circus Maximus stadium. Driving these wild horses in a straight line and getting them to work together round the corners without overturning the chariot takes real skill. If he allows them to slow down, he'll lose the race; he needs their energy to win. But if he doesn't harness that energy, then chariot, horses and rider will all go crashing into the barriers and out of the race.

A parent's task is the same: to tame the will without breaking the spirit. Punishment, like discipline in general, should be used to harness and guide a child's spirit and energy constructively. All punishment should be:

- **Fair.** If a punishment isn't fair, your child will learn nothing about self-control and responsibility from it. All they'll learn is that you're unfair. As a result, they'll feel angry, rejected, and misunderstood – all emotions guaranteed to produce more bad behaviour in future. By taking a short cut, not thinking, and being unfair in the punishment you hand out, you'll only end up adding to your problems and giving yourself a much bigger battle to fight later on – by which time they'll respect you a lot less. But being fair doesn't necessarily mean doling out the same punishment to each child who commits the same offence. Different children react in different ways. A sensitive child may learn their lesson simply by being given a stern talking to, whilst further action may be needed for a more 'hardened' child.

- **Firm.** Make sure your 'No' means no and your 'Yes' means yes. If you mean 'No', say it and stick to it, or all you'll teach your kids is that they can get whatever they want if they're prepared to grind you down for long enough. In other words, they'll end up believing that tantrums and other forms of disobedience work provided they're dedicated enough to stick at it. So choose your battles carefully, and make sure you stand your ground when it matters.

- **Consistent.** Don't allow your moods to influence your decisions about punishment. If something is wrong, it's wrong, however tired you are. The boundaries must always be there. If an offence is treated as trivial one week and serious the next, your child will end up confused about where and what the boundaries really are. That's why it's always good to have a short 'cooling off period' before you take any action, even if it's just a few minutes. It'll give you time to get hold of yourself, assess the situation and think about a suitable punishment. What's more, it might even give your child enough time to realise what they've done wrong, and calm down or apologise.

Top Tip: *Unless your punishments are **fair**, **firm** and **consistent**, they won't harness your child's energy constructively.*

Spoilt for Choice

In the cupboard under the stairs in our house is a big metal box filled with tools. When Cornelia and I first got married, this box was smaller and virtually empty. But gradually the number of tools it contained grew as I found I never had the right tool to do the job that needed doing around the house. So over the years, I've added an assorted collection of spanners, sockets, saws, Allen keys, tape measures, screwdrivers, chisels, pliers and wrenches. I may not be 'Mr DIY', but I know you can't fix everything with a hammer!

And punishment is exactly the same. You can't do the whole job with just one tool – especially if it's a hammer! A wise parent understands the need to use a wide variety of disciplinary tools, sensitively choosing the right one for each occasion – one that fits both the 'crime' and the child. There's lots of scope for flexibility here. Smacking, for example, whilst a no-go area for many parents, is considered by others to be *one* of these tools. But even for those parents who do believe in it, it's one that's best used very sparingly. Alternative punishments to smacking fall into three basic categories:

- **Verbal tellings-off:** a serious talk in a serious voice will some-

35

times have the desired effect. Your kids want you to be pleased with them, so letting them know they've disappointed you can be extremely effective.

- **Sending children to a 'cooling off' place:** e.g., their bedroom or a corner of the room. (But make sure it's a real punishment: a friend of mine *loved* being sent to his room, where he could do what he wanted!) One couple I know send their kids half way up the stairs for half an hour whenever they're naughty. They say it's effective because there's nothing for them to do there except think about what they did wrong.

- **Withdrawing privileges:** including the removal of pocket money or treats, not being allowed to stay up late at weekends, limiting the use of computers or other toys, banning favourite TV programmes, grounding and other restrictions.

 Top Tip: Choose a punishment that's right for both the 'crime' and the child who's committed it!

Spare the Rod?

Smacking is a big issue. An expert once explained on TV how smacking was a violation of human rights, likely to leave a child needing therapy. 'We've got to *talk* through the problems instead,' she concluded. Her interviewer was unconvinced: 'Perhaps a good smack is the right therapy sometimes,' she quipped. Who's right? Is smacking a form of punishment whose time is past? Does it scar children emotionally for life and teach them that violence is the way to solve their problems? Or can it have a positive effect, helping them develop the self-discipline they need?

Some people argue that smacking is wrong because, unlike other kinds of punishment, it's violent and abusive. But the truth is that shouting and screaming uncontrollably at a child can be every bit as abusive and emotionally scarring as an uncaring smack or slap. A few years ago, the director of one infamous children's home was sacked not just for beating the children in his care, but equally for using a system known as 'pin-down', where he confined them to their rooms for days at a time. The children considered this kind of 'solitary confinement' even more abusive than being beaten.

The problem, in other words, isn't confined to smacking. It goes far deeper than that. It's actually about the way in which *any* punishment is given. There's a world of difference between tapping a toddler lightly on the wrist and giving a ten-year-old an angry slap or a prolonged thrashing with a belt. In fact, lumping these together under one label – 'smacking' – as if they were all the same, is extremely misleading.

The truth is that *any* punishment given as an unthought-out, arbitrary or even violent reaction is abusive. Any punishment that's undisciplined and handed out in the heat of the moment is bound to be damaging. This kind of punishment will confuse and scar a child emotionally. And, just as importantly, it won't work. But the double tragedy with out-of-control smacking is that the already devastating impact of emotional scarring and damage caused by undisciplined discipline is added to by physical pain and abuse.

Top Tip: *Any punishment can be violent and abusive if given in an angry or unthought-out way.*

The Last Word

The last word, after any punishment, must always be positive. It's vital for your child to know they've done wrong, but it's every bit as important for them to know that you love them anyway. So do your best to let them know that you're *only* punishing them because you love them. Otherwise they may think you only love them when they're being good. And that, of course, is the exact opposite of the message you want to send.

My dad's favourite phrase when he had to punish me was, 'This'll hurt me a lot more than it hurts you!' Not surprisingly, I didn't believe him at the time. But as I've grown older, with children of my own, I've come to see he was telling the truth. A good parent is bound to agonise over the punishment, but knows they have to act rather than turn a blind eye. It's always painful for them to punish their child. But in the end, they love them too much to let them get away with doing something destructive and wrong.

 Top Tip: *Love and discipline your child – just don't expect them to jump for joy and thank you for it at the time!*

'I Can Fit You In Next Thursday'

How Do I Make Time for My Child?

Roy Castle, the popular entertainer, gave a press conference shortly before he died. The lung cancer that eventually claimed his life was already well advanced. A reporter asked him, 'How does it feel to know that you only have a few months to live?' There was an awkward silence. Everyone wanted to know the answer, but no one else had dared to ask the question. Then Roy smiled and said very softly, 'If I knew I had a few months to live, I'd be unique. You don't even know if you'll still be alive this time tomorrow.'

Most of us assume we'll be around for years to come, so we order our priorities accordingly. We put off doing *important* things because we're frankly too busy trying to do all the *urgent* things that keep piling up. We assume there'll be time to get round to the important things later on. We work all hours in order to get a promotion at work and tell ourselves that one day there'll be more time to collect conkers, watch our son play football, help our daughter with her homework, or read them a bedtime story.

But if we thought we only had a year to live, most of us would look at life differently. After all, as the famous saying goes, 'Nobody ever said on their deathbed, "I wish I'd spent more time at the office"'. So why do so many of us – men and women – act as if work were more important than our family? And why do the rest of us so often allow the housework and endless other 'commitments' to tire us out and get between us and our child?

Top Tip: Life is unpredictable, so don't put off making time for your child.

Carpe Diem! Seize the Day!

Children don't ask to be born. They're not around to be consulted. Deliberately or not, we invite our kids into our lives. This means that, once they're here, we *owe* them the time, security, love and care they desperately need in order to thrive. From the moment they're born, we're effectively in debt to our children.

But more than that, the years you've got with your kids are short and irreplaceable. I once interviewed the famous American, Dr Billy Graham. Taking advantage of meeting one of the most famous men of the twentieth century, I asked him what advice he had about making the most of life. I expected him to say something so deep it would take me months to get to grips with its full meaning, so I geared myself up and leant in close to make sure I caught every word. There was a long silence that seemed to go on for ever. Then he said, 'Life goes a lot quicker than you expect it to, so use each day wisely.' That was it.

But it's true. There aren't many summer holidays, Bonfire nights, Easter bunny hunts, Pancake Days, conker collecting sessions and Christmas Eves left when your child will still want to be with you. So a wise parent needs to grasp every opportunity during these fleeting early years with both hands. Seize the day because your child will soon be gone.

There'll come a day when they won't ask you to read to them any more, or want to sit on your lap and fall asleep, or play football with you, or get you to mend their bike. And strange as it may seem, all the things you struggle with now, you'll long for then. There'll be days when you desperately want to read them a story – every word, all the way through! You'll wonder why you ever found reading *The Bumper Book of Bedtime Stories* (for the twenty-seventh time) so boring that you cheated and turned over three pages at once.

The years you have with your child will be over and gone before you know it. Though it seems like only yesterday when I first held her in my arms, my eldest child may leave home for college just two years from now. I'd do well to remind myself of this every time she asks me to do something with her, or wants to talk, or just wants us to sit and watch TV together.

I may feel that I can't really afford the time to meet all my kid's demands. In light of all the other calls made on me, helping them with their homework or taking them to see a film may not seem to come high on my list of priorities. But the boot will soon be on the other foot. One day, in the not too distant future, *I'll* be the one phoning to ask if they're too busy to pop home for the weekend.

Rather than me finding time for them, they'll be trying (I hope!) to fit *me* into their hectic schedule and busy social diary.

 Top Tip: Life is shorter than you think, so invest time in your child's life whilst you still can.

Work Time

'Time is money,' quipped Benjamin Franklin. But in fact, time is far more valuable than money. The person with lots of time but no money has everything to play for. But the person with lots of money and no time is dead! The truth is, of course, that it's not easy for most of us to find time for our kids. Even those who work in the home as a full-time mum or dad often find that all the domestic chores take up so much time that there's very little left at the end just to sit down and be with their children.

A business consultant once came across a farmer resting under a tree. 'You should work harder, plant more,' he told him. 'Then you'd have more crops to sell, and you could hire people to do the work for you.' 'What would I do then?' asked the farmer. 'Sit back and take things easy,' said the consultant. 'But that's what I'm doing now,' replied the farmer.

It's easy to blame your job or the housework for your lack of time to spend with your child. It's also easy, especially if you're a working mother, to get trapped into feeling really guilty about spending time at work, away from your kids. But contrary to popular opinion, the major tensions that arise because of competing home and work pressures aren't really anything to do with the type of job or responsibilities you or your partner has. They're actually more to do with you and your *personality*.

It took me a long time to realise this. My workaholic tendencies have little or nothing to do with what I do for a living. Instead, they're part of *me*. I'd have been just as busy if I'd become a banker, plumber, journalist, salesman, gardener, milkman, doctor or lawyer. It's uncomfortable to admit it, but when we blame 'work' for our failure to give our family the time and support they need, we're kidding ourselves. I'm not trying to dismiss work pressures. I know all too well how real they can be. It's just that going *out* to work doesn't excuse anyone from coming *home* to work.

Those of us who work outside the home can't just decide to turn off once we're inside the front door. However much we might want to, we can't just put our feet up in front of the TV and switch off. I can't excuse myself from involvement with my family and my share of the chores on the grounds that I've been 'working hard all day'. It's a fatal mistake for someone in paid employment to behave as though 'work' stops the moment they leave the site or finish sifting through papers. The truth is that we need to work every bit as hard at our home life as we do in our workplace. What's more, making an effort at home isn't just the right thing to do – it's actually rewarding!

 Top Tip: *It's not your work that stops you spending time with your child – it's **you**!*

43

The One and Only

Of course, balancing family and work is never easy. But then, it isn't easy finding time to mix a passion for work with a passion for swimming, football, bowling, fishing, golf or even the pub, club or gym — yet busy men and women have managed it for years. The very undramatic truth is that the decisions *can* be made — if we're willing to make them. As they say, 'Where there's a will, there's a way'. Our children *need* our time. And if it mattered enough to us, we'd find it for them. That's the uncomfortable truth, no matter how valid our excuses sound.

The trouble is, we often fail to grasp just how important our attention is to them. And of course, one of the main reasons for this mistake is that we don't spend enough time with them for it to become obvious to us. It's a catch-22 situation. Giving our children time is a low priority for us because we don't spend long enough with them to realise how much they need. And because it's a low priority, we never have the time to discover that we need to change our priorities.

For Simon, the first clue that he wasn't spending enough time with his seven-year-old son, Ben, came one Christmas Eve. Sneaking into Ben's room a few minutes before midnight, clutching a stocking that was bursting with presents, he found a letter addressed to Santa Claus at the foot of the bed, next to one of his son's favourite toys. He picked up the letter, put the stocking in its place, and went back to the living room. Later, anxious to see what Ben had asked for, he opened the letter and started reading. 'Dear Santa,' it said, 'thank you for coming all the way to see me. I don't want anything this year. Mummy and daddy give me lots of toys. Please can you wake me up instead? I want to talk to you. I've got some important questions to ask you about. Mummy and daddy have very important jobs. They are very busy, so I can't ask them. Thank you. Yours sincerely, Ben. PS: who does *your* stocking? Here's one of my toys. Don't worry, I have lots.'

Most of us like to think we're pretty important at work. Some of us even risk getting mesmerised by our self-importance. But don't fool yourself: however crucial you think you are at work, someone else can, and eventually will, take your place. It's hard to admit it, but you're *not* indispensible. Except, that is, at home. You're the only mum or dad your child has got. They *want* and *need* to spend time with you. And like it or not, how you're doing at work isn't a big priority for them. What you do *for them* is far more important. They don't care about your promotion, your profile or the size of your pay packet. But they *do* care about you, and need to know that you care about *them*. So make time for them while you still can, before the opportunities are gone for ever.

 Top Tip: *You're irreplaceable in your child's life, so make them a priority.*

'I've Pencilled You In for between the News and the Weather ...'

There's no secret formula for balancing all the competing demands life throws at you and making the quantity and quality of time your child needs. It's like walking a tight-rope. It's not a case of struggling initially to get your balance and then, having done so, finding yourself free to carry on regardless. Staying upright on the high wire involves making *continual* tiny – but absolutely vital – adjustments.

In the 1980s, it was fashionable to think that it didn't really matter *how much* time you spent with your kids so long as it was 'quality time'. People convinced themselves that if they set aside short bursts of 'power time' with their children – filled with intense, quality activity – they'd have fulfilled their obligation as a parent. But it doesn't work like that. One of the clearest ways children have of measuring the *quality* of time we spend with them is by looking at its sheer *quantity*.

Actually, this makes a lot of sense. After all, when you love someone, you want to spend as much time with them as you can. So if your child gets the impression you don't want to spend time with them, it's logical for them to assume that you don't really love them, whatever else you might tell them or give them. Your child needs your *presence*, not your *presents*. (Though it won't matter *how* much time you spend with your child if, in doing so, you still give them the impression you don't really want them around.)

Important conversations rarely happen on cue. When someone asks how you are, what do you say? 'OK.' It's the standard reply, even if it's untrue. Few of us wear our hearts on our sleeves. For most of us, it takes a lot of courage to open up and tell someone our innermost thoughts, feelings or problems. And it's the same for children. Trust is built slowly over time. The deep issues and big questions trickle out because a parent is *there*. In fact, kids have a habit of asking the deepest questions at the most inappropriate times. Every now and then – as you're making the tea, fixing something, or just watching TV – they'll raise all sorts of unexpected and important subjects 'out of the blue'.

Most of the best conversations I've had with my kids about careers, racism, bullying, love, failure, success, honesty, relationships, money, justice, etc., have started like this. Just being around your child sends them the message, 'I'm comfortable with you. I enjoy your company. I'm glad you're here.' And they're reassured that it's safe for them to ask intimate questions or talk about personal things without fear of rejection.

 Top Tip: Invest **quantity** time if you want to reap **quality** conversation.

Getting Family Fit

Of course, knowing all this is one thing, but actually making the time is another. It's rather like sport. We all want to be fit, strong and healthy. But for most of us, being out of shape is a habit we'll never change, for one simple reason: we don't get up at six every morning and put in the effort to do the training.

One commentator described the 1996 Olympic Games in Atlanta as an event where 'the world's fittest performed for the world's fattest'. And a British doctor warned that the public were more at risk from the onset of 'Mad Couch Disease' than Mad

Cow Disease. 'Spectating is now by far the most popular and dangerous sport there is,' he added. As a nation, we spend hours in front of the TV watching *others* take exercise rather than taking it ourselves. It's true what they say about football: twenty-two thousand people in need of exercise watch twenty-two people in need of a rest! But in exactly the same way, many of us settle for being spectators in our children's lives.

Making time for your family requires the same kind of dedicated, disciplined effort and activity as training for sport. The problem is, so many good intentions fall flat because the goals we set ourselves are overly ambitious. Just as you shouldn't start trying to get fit by pledging to run a half-marathon every morning, so it's equally daft to promise to make dramatic changes to your lifestyle overnight. Even if you manage an initial burst of enthusiasm, you're unlikely to keep it going in the long run. It's better to get 'family fit' slowly, in a well disciplined but not overly demanding way.

Don't bite off more than you can chew, promising to make unrealistic changes to your diary or working habits. As all successful business people know, goals must be realistic and sensible. Rather than trying to get home from work two hours earlier every day, try to get home just thirty minutes earlier, twice a week, to read your child a story before they go to bed. Rather than pledging to spend every night in and take every weekend off to be with your child, ring-fence just one night a week and one weekend a month as uninterruptable family time when you do something together. The secret is, start small but make it a priority. Apply the same dedication to achieving your objective at home as you would to an objective at work.

Top Tip: *Be disciplined – make spending time with your child a firm priority.*

Firm Foundations

When you spend time with your child, you help create good family memories for them – memories that will play a huge part in establishing their security and stability, or lack of it, later on. The truth is, memories that remind people they're loved create a powerful emotional base on which to build the rest of their lives. Wherever they go and whatever they do, these memories will help provide them with an unshakeable feeling of security.

I've slowly learnt that it's easier to set time aside for my family and not allow other things to get in the way if we plan to do something specific: treats, outings, holidays or surprises. I've also learnt that what we do isn't half as important as the fact that we do it together. It doesn't matter if it's camping in the back garden, playing snooker, having a weekend away, eating out, driving to the seaside, playing tennis, watching football, playing Monopoly or any of a thousand and one other activities. By taking the time to do *something* together as a family, and to enjoy each other's company, we're cementing relationships, building good memories, and proving to our children that our love is more than words.

A couple of summers ago, Cornelia and I arranged a treasure hunt for our kids while we were on holiday. We bought some inexpensive 'treasure' we knew they'd like, wrote a series of clues, and

49

hid them in the house and fields around where we were staying. Solving Clue One led them to Clue Two, and so on. When the end of the trail was finally reached, they were all happy with the spoils of their hard work. But the best thing is that, long after the 'treasure' has been lost or broken, the memory of a happy childhood day will live on.

But it's also important to spend time with each child individually. I often take one or another of our children to breakfast on Saturdays at McDonalds. It's cheap and cheerful, but it's a great time to talk by ourselves, laugh, tell jokes and catch up on things without all the distractions of home. Occasionally I take one of our daughters out on a 'date' to a restaurant somewhere, or book to go to a football match with one of the boys. (Try as I might, I just can't get our girls interested in supporting Crystal Palace!) It doesn't need to cost the earth. You don't have to take your kids to the Ritz to make it special. You just have to take the time. As they say, kids spell 'love' T-I-M-E.

And the funny thing is, however reluctant you are to do it at first, you'll probably end up enjoying it even more than they do.

 Top Tip: *Give your child a childhood worth remembering – build good memories for them now.*

'It's Not Fair!'

How Can I Create a Happy Family?

We've all seen them on TV, and they make us sick. Hollywood pictures of happy, healthy, low-fat, low-cholesterol, all-singing, all-dancing, minty-fresh families with perfect smiles and pure white teeth, laughing, joking, talking and eating balanced breakfasts together in hygienic, fully fitted kitchens in wonderfully decorated, brightly furnished, spacious homes. The sun is shining, the birds are singing, the freshly squeezed orange juice is flowing, and everyone is looking forward to another glorious day in Paradise.

I don't know about you, but our house is different. Everyone is late and everything is rushed. I can't find my shoes, one of the kids can't find their homework, and the milk gets spilled over the kitchen table. A bitter argument breaks out over who's going to have the free plastic dinosaur in the cornflakes packet, and who had it last time. Someone steps on the cat. Cornelia and I can't quite agree on who last had the car keys. I'm convinced it was her, and point out that she's always losing things and it's about time she got a grip on herself – until, that is, I find them in my coat pocket and accuse one of the kids of putting them there.

If any of this sounds familiar, you may be wondering why – in spite of all your plans to make everything just perfect – your house and homelife closely resemble a war zone. The reason is simple: you're human. That means you're not a perfect parent, your kids aren't perfect children, and your family is never going to be one of those perfect, plastic Hollywood families. In fact, perfect happy families simply don't exist. The truth is that breakfast is almost *always* a war zone – even in Hollywood!

If we fall for the lie that there's a happy family with no real problems just down the road, we're bound to end up demoralised when we can't live up to their standard. But in reality, behind their smartly painted front doors, all families have the same troubles, tensions, squabbles and dilemmas as you do. As they say, the grass may be greener 'over there', but it still needs mowing!

Top Tip: There's no such thing as a perfect happy family, so don't wear yourself out trying to create one!

Happy Ever After?

If perfection isn't possible, happiness certainly is. The only snag is that you have to work a lot harder than you might think to achieve it. When Thomas Jefferson drafted the American Declaration of Independence in June 1776, he suggested that among people's 'unalienable rights' were, 'life, liberty and the *pursuit* of happiness', because unlike so many of us, who've been trained by films or fairy stories to expect that things will automatically end 'happily ever after', Jefferson knew that happiness didn't just fall into people's laps. They had to work at *pursuing* it.

Speaking at the end of the hippy era, former Beatles star John Lennon admitted that he and his friends had been naïve to think that they could solve all the world's problems by sitting around singing 'All You Need Is Love' and 'Give Peace a Chance'. But the real problem wasn't that they overestimated the vital importance of love and peace; it was that they had a very rose-tinted, fluffy, floaty idea of what love and peace were. The truth is that love and peace are extremely tough and costly to attain or sustain, as the struggle of two famous peace campaigners – Gandhi and Martin Luther King – had already proved to the world.

Almost all families love each other, but that doesn't necessarily translate itself into peace and harmony in the home. The closeness of family life has a way of catching us off guard, getting under our skin and making us lose our cool over the wrong things. Minor incidents get turned into full-scale dramas. Brothers and sisters wind each other up and run each other down at the slightest provocation. A debate over the tiniest thing can rapidly escalate into something closely resembling nuclear meltdown.

Problems don't automatically resolve themselves, so it takes a lot of patience, hard work, humility and discipline to make and keep the family peace.

 Top Tip: *Peace and happiness don't come automatically. You have to work at them.*

The Whole Story

Always look before you leap. Whatever you do, resist the temptation to jump straight in with both feet to sort out trouble between your children. Though some squabbles are just what they appear to be, the majority aren't. More often than not, fights between siblings are a case of six of one and half a dozen of the other. That means that if you take things at face value, you run the risk of being unfair, and that's bound gradually to undermine your authority and relationship with them all.

When David's younger son rang him at work, he knew something was wrong. It was the school holidays, and his two sons were home with their older sister. 'John kicked the ball into next door's garden and won't get it back,' Paul explained. They were always kicking the ball into next door's garden, so David had devised a simple rule: whoever kicks the ball over has to fetch it back. It was clear what had to be done. He called John to the phone and was to the point: 'You kicked the ball over. You get it back. No excuses.'

When he got home that evening, David was immediately greeted by Paul telling him that John still *refused* to get the ball back. His patience stretched thin, David took decisive action. He frog-marched John next door and forced him to pick up the ball. But when they got back to the kitchen, David's daughter explained what had *really* happened. The two boys had been kicking the ball around in the back garden when Paul had let fly a shot that was undoubtedly headed straight over the fence – the fourth to head that way in ten minutes! In a desperate bid to stop it, John had managed to get a foot to it, but not enough to prevent the inevitable. Being only seven, Paul had immediately denied responsibility. And when John had refused to get the ball, he'd phoned David.

If David had asked John to get the ball anyway, regardless of blame, things might have turned out differently. But because he hadn't bothered to find out the whole story before reaching a decision, he'd not only treated John unfairly, he'd also made him think that he didn't trust him. By the time his daughter had finished talking, David realised he had some big apologies to make.

Always remember: when you're 100 per cent sure you're right, you're 80 per cent likely to be wrong. So rather than jumping to hasty conclusions, do what you can to unearth both sides of the story before you make up your mind about who's right and who's wrong – or you may come to regret it later.

Top Tip: *Don't act until you've heard both sides of the story and had a chance to think.*

Hothouse Flowers

Correctly determining blame may be important, but it isn't the end of the road. The really big question is, *why* is one of your children choosing to pick on another in the first place? Are they misbehaving because they're worried about something? Are they being bullied themselves, and simply taking out their frustrations on brothers or sisters who aren't really to blame? Or is it simply that they're consciously flexing their muscles and trying it on? Discovering the underlying issue is likely to take time and thought, but it is essential. It's extremely short-sighted simply to make your children 'kiss and make up'. The problem will only recur unless you identify and deal with the root cause. Just like weeds in the garden, if you don't pull them up by their roots, they'll come back stronger than ever.

Some problems are straightforward, and you can take them at face value. But just as often, the underlying tensions and difficulties are far deeper and harder to spot. Many of the fights that happen between brothers and sisters are more to do with personal issues they're facing than with *inter*personal ones. The problem is that, in the hothouse environment of a family, one child may not feel they have the space they need to deal with personal pressures, tensions and worries without causing massive disruption to other family members. The truth is that, however spacious your house, your family's a confined group, which means that you're bound to take out your problems on someone else eventually.

The only real way to get to the roots of sibling tensions is to spend *time* with your children – but not just when there's a crisis. For instance, if the only time you take your children out for a chat and a bite to eat is when there's something wrong, they'll never learn to relax on their own with you. They won't trust you enough to open up to you. So it's an investment: by talking things through with each child on their own on a regular basis (rather than just when there's an obvious crisis), you'll get to appreciate what they're going through. You'll also get to understand a lot more about the kinds of tension they're under, which will help you more readily anticipate some of the problems and crisis points before they arise, and take steps to deal with them ahead of time.

Sometimes all your child needs to resolve their problems is a parent-shaped sounding board – someone who will listen to and understand them. Being able to offload their worries on to you provides them with a vital pressure valve, releasing some of the tension that might otherwise slowly build up and then boil over on to one of their brothers or sisters in a far less constructive way. Often they will be only too eager to soak up some good advice about how to handle tough situations (though you shouldn't always expect them to acknowledge it there and then!). And always, without fail, even when they're being cold toward you, they need to know that you love them and value them for who they are, with no strings attached.

Spending time alone with each of your children gives them an opportunity to talk about what's bothering them. But it also shows them that you love *them* enough to want to spend time specifically with *them* rather than only as part of the family group because they happen to belong to it. Don't forget: the way to make each child *feel* like they matter is for each child *to* matter, and that takes a commitment of your time.

Top Tip: *Spending time with your children individually will help you deal with tensions before they reach crisis point.*

'Between These Four Walls ...'

Your task as a parent is to prepare and equip your children for the day when you're not there any more and they have to make decisions on their own. That means it's far better to help them resolve their *own* problems than to impose your endless solutions on them. For one thing, most squabbles between brothers and sisters resolve themselves anyway – it's just a matter of time. But more importantly, if they always come to rely on *you* to settle their disputes for them, they'll never learn to take responsibility and sort them out for themselves. As the saying goes, 'Give someone a fish and they have food for a day; *teach* them to fish and they have food for a lifetime'.

My friend Sophie is two years younger than her brother Alan. Although they get on great now, they fought like cat and dog as children. At ten, Sophie was a good deal smaller than Alan. As a result, she always ended up losing. When it finally dawned on her she'd never beat him physically, she changed tack. Instead of arguing when he said something provocative, which inevitably led to bruises, she started to ignore him. But Sophie says that her new strategy was a complete disaster – an instant failure. Alan hated being ignored even more than he hated being contradicted, and Sophie ended up with even bigger bruises than before.

When she complained to her mum, her mum gave her some advice. 'He only hits you because he doesn't know how to admit he's wrong. So ask yourself if it's worth getting a bruise over. If not, give in. Don't get dragged down to his level – keep your dignity. Tell yourself that he'll grow out of it, but don't hit back. In fact, be deliberately nice and polite to him. Believe me, you'll feel a *lot* better and you'll defuse him just like that.'

Giving in isn't always an option, of course. Sometimes your kids will have to stand their ground. Sometimes it *is* worth getting a bruise over. In fact, one of the most important skills you can teach your children about resolving their differences with other people is knowing when they can afford to back down and when they can't. Just as *you* need to choose carefully which battles you have to fight – and win – with your kids in order to give them the self-discipline they need, so they need to learn how to pick their battles carefully with other people.

There are times, of course, when you *have* to step in and get involved, because one or other of your children is in danger of getting hurt. But whenever you can, teach your children how to resolve their own differences and resist the temptation automatically to leap in to devise solutions for them.

Top Tip: *Try to resolve your children's rows **with** them, not **for** them.*

The Right Tool for the Right Job

One of the biggest causes of friction in our house used to be the computer. We had four children and only one computer, and whichever way you calculate it, four into one just doesn't go! We had a rota system which gave each child an allocated 'slot' in the evening when the computer was reserved for their use, and at first it worked well. But as the older ones started having to use the computer more and more for school work, they couldn't guarantee finishing in the allotted time and things got difficult.

In this case, the solution was simple: we saved up about £400, and a couple of years ago splashed out on another computer – a slightly outdated second-hand one, but still up to the job – which we gave to Emily, our eldest child, who was working hard on her GCSEs. That way she had the time she needed on her own computer, and her time slot on the main family computer could be divided equally between the others.

Sometimes family tensions can be resolved using this kind of practical solution. If the underlying problem is a practical one, the solution will have to be equally 'hands-on'. It doesn't always have to cost the earth, of course. A few years ago, Sally was at her wits' end about what to do with her two sons, Mike and Tim, who were always fighting. At first she thought it was simply a passing phase – they were six and eight – but the fights just kept on getting worse. In the end, she took drastic action. The two had always shared a room, in spite of the fact that the family lived in a small, three-bedroom terraced house. The tiny third bedroom had been her husband's 'office' until the arrival of Amy, their daughter, four years before. After that it became her nursery, and then her bedroom.

When Sally moved Amy in with Mike, giving the third room to Tim, things instantly improved. Tim felt grown up because he had his own room, no matter how small it was; Mike felt grown up because, though he still had to share, he was now *big* brother in the room, not *little* brother; and Amy felt grown up because she was old enough to live in the 'big room', which was far more exciting than her old one. Anyway, she didn't really like being on her own at night. Sally knows this solution will only last a few years, but it's a few years of relative peace – while they save for a loft conversion!

Top Tip: *If it's a practical problem, try to find a practical answer.*

Separate But Equal

The one thing guaranteed to produce an unhappy home is when parents seem to love one child more than another. It's vital for all your children to know you love them equally and *unconditionally*, for who they are and with no strings attached.

Equal treatment, however, doesn't necessarily mean *identical* treatment. Some things will obviously be the same across the board: not getting down from the table before a meal is over, not lying, not trampling mud through the house, being polite, always saying 'please' and 'thank you', always doing their homework on time, going to bed at the right time, etc. But a lot of things will vary because your children are different from one another: they have different personalities and different ages, for a start. That means that, although the desired end-result may be the same, how you go about achieving it will differ from child to child.

Gavin was very bright, good-looking and a hard working all-rounder at school. To encourage him, his mum and dad cheered him on at every stage. But sadly, they came to expect the same kind of success all round from his sister Kate. Two years younger than Gavin, Kate had neither his looks nor his brains. In fact, she didn't appear to excel at anything. To give her 'something to aspire to', they constantly compared her progress with Gavin's – which made her feel like an even bigger failure than ever. 'If only you were more like your brother,' they told her. But no matter how hard she tried, she knew she'd never match her brother.

Telling a child that you wish they were more like their brother or sister is a guaranteed way to humiliate them, destroying their self-esteem and self-worth – not to mention their relationship with their brother or sister! If Kate's parents had spent more time with her individually, finding out what she was good at and measuring her performance against her *own* potential rather than her brother's, they'd have built up a completely different picture of her, and would have tried to motivate and discipline her very differently to her brother. As a result, she'd have felt equally and fairly treated by them. But by trying to use an identical yardstick for both their children, irrespective of their unique strengths and weaknesses, Kate's parents made her feel unfairly treated and hardly loved at all.

The only way to ensure being fair with each of your children is to spend time with them and make sure you know their strengths and weaknesses. There's no substitute for this. It's the only way to find out and deal with what's causing disruptive behaviour, and it's the only way to give your children the absolute assurance of the love they need to cope with all that life will throw at them.

 Top Tip: *'Equal' doesn't always mean 'identical' in the way you treat your children, so take time getting to know them as individuals.*

PART TWO: SCHOOL

Partners Together

What Should I Expect from My Child's Teachers?

'Unteachable – that's what they used to call my son,' complained the lady whose voice boomed out at me as I turned on the radio this morning. 'I was always going down to the school to stick up for him,' she continued. 'The teachers said he was a troublemaker but I wasn't having any of that! I used to get mad. It wasn't his fault. He was being set up – provoked.' Then she paused. 'But the thing is, I've got to admit it, he's just so different now. Ever since I went on that course for parents, I've felt so much more in control. And his behaviour has been transformed. I now realise that his problems were never really *his* problems, or even the school's problems. They were mine. That's all there is to it.'

School isn't an Adult Machine. It's not a factory that processes children into fresh, vibrant, productive members of society. For that

63

matter, neither are the Boy Scouts, Girl Guides, Army Training Corps, Sunday School, snooker hall, football club, Cake Bake Club or Margaret Whiffle Academy for Young Ladies. They can all play an important role in partnership with the family, but no one else can do a parent's job. And no one else should. The responsibility for producing mature, well-motivated, independent, creative, adult members of society belongs not to the school, the media or wider society – though these will help or hinder – but to parents. The buck stops here!

In other words, you can't just ship your child off to school in the morning and expect them to perform a miracle without you. Parents and teachers work in partnership with each other in the task of transforming children into adults.

Top Tip: *Don't pass the buck – schools are there to bring up your child **with** you, not **for** you!*

Top Dog

The truth is that the partnership between parents and teachers is an *unequal* one, where the school plays a supporting role to the parents, not the other way round! There are several reasons for this.

For one thing, you're the most influential role model your child has. For the first eight to ten years of their lives, they actively want to walk, talk, look, sound, think and act like you. You're their hero. Like it or not, they learn a huge amount just by watching what you do and say and copying it. No matter how influential your child's teachers may be, they'll never have the influence you do. No one can replace you, even if they wanted to. As far as your child is concerned, you're the best in the universe.

What's more, although it may not always seem like it, your child spends more time with you than with their teachers. Of the 6,574 days they have between their birth and their eighteenth birthday, they'll spend on average just 2,145 of them – less than a third – at school. And even during term, they'll only spend about a third of the day at school. The rest of it they spend with you, or those you choose to delegate the responsibility to for looking after them. So as far as their time goes, whether you make the most of it or not, the fact is that you're the major shareholder in your child's life. It's up to you to make the right investment.

> **Top Tip:** You're the biggest influence in your child's life, so don't waste the opportunity.

Apple for Teacher

But if your child does spend 2,145 days of their life in school, it's absolutely vital for you to take a very active interest in what happens there. You just can't afford to ignore what they're doing or learning. In fact, *they* can't afford for you to ignore it either. From homework to sports days, reports to parents' evenings, your child needs to know that you're not just solidly behind their efforts to learn at school, but also solidly behind the school's efforts to teach them. By taking an interest in what your child does for seven hours of the day, you're sending them the message that school and their education are important.

And the school needs to know that too! The teachers need to know the job they're trying to do during the day is being reinforced, not undermined, when your child gets home. In practical terms, that means talking with them if there's a problem, comparing notes, being honest at parents' evenings and ensuring your child gets on with their homework and any other assignments they've been set, delivering them on time. There's nothing worse for a teacher than to feel that their hard work is being systematically eroded by a child's home environment.

Of course, none of this means you need to buy a dentist's chair, a video camera and a high-powered lighting rig in order to give your child a convincing interrogation at the end of every school day! In fact, the more your 'healthy interest' comes to resemble the 'third degree', the less effective it is. Mechanically asking your child how their day was when they've just got through the door is probably not a good idea. Just like you, after a hard day, they may need to relax and put their feet up for half an hour or so first.

Why not test yourself? How much do you really know about what your child does all day? Casually make it your business to find out.

- Who's their favourite teacher?
- What's their favourite lesson?
- What are they learning in history at the moment?
- What project are they working on?
- How's the football team doing?
- What do they like most about school?

- What *don't* they enjoy about it?
- What's their worst subject, and why?
- Who are their friends?

If you don't know the answers to these questions, start finding out now!

Top Tip: *Take an active interest in your child's education – but avoid the 'third degree'.*

'Don't Leave It to the Last Minute'

If your child is old enough to be given homework, your job is to play that vital role of helping them develop the necessary self-discipline to get it done – on time and up to standard. The older they get, the more important homework will become for them, and the longer it'll take to do. What may start out at twenty minutes for a ten-year-old could easily become two to three hours by the time they're sixteen and up to their eyeballs in either GCSE coursework or, worse still, that dreaded but necessary evil, revision.

So never be tempted to see homework as a trivial thing. Whatever their age, it's vital for them to learn to do, or at least tackle, what's set as best they can. They may complain about having to do it before they're allowed to watch TV or play with their friends, and *you* may even start to wonder what's so important about it. But by helping them cope with the discipline of sitting down and completing the tasks that have been set for them, you're enabling them to develop a skill that'll make the difference between success or failure when it finally comes to GCSEs, A levels and further education.

In the film *The Karate Kid*, a young boy is promised karate lessons by an old expert. At first he's keen to learn everything the old man has to teach him, but he soon becomes disillusioned. Rather than teaching him karate, the old man just gets him to do chores: paint the fence, sweep the floor or scrub the patio. Not only that, but he's extremely fussy about how each task should be done: long up and down movements or tiny circular ones. In the end, the boy has had enough and complains. But to his surprise, the old man smiles – and shows him how each of the 'chores' is really a karate movement. Without realising it, he's been rehearsing these movements over and over again until they're so ingrained they've become a habit.

If it's the school's responsibility to give them homework, it's your task to help make sure they do it, instilling the habit and self-discipline into them. So help your child devise a schedule or timetable to achieve the task. Sit down with them and find out how much work they regularly have to do, then fit that into 'slots' around fixed events like getting home from school and having dinner. And don't worry about them missing their favourite TV programmes: that's what video recorders were invented for!

It may be a good idea to let your child have a bit of relaxation time when they first get home from school, before they get started, and to organise the work into manageable thirty-minute chunks, with a short break in between each one. Help them to see that, though it's very appealing, putting off the hardest bits till the end isn't very wise – they'll just be far more tired and the work will seem even tougher. Instead, it makes sense to timetable their worst subjects in first and save the easy bits to the end. And at the week-end, help them see that tackling their homework on Friday night or Saturday morning is a better option than leaving it until a last-minute panic on Sunday night.

Until they've got the habit, their bedroom may not be the best place to work, as it's likely to be filled with too many distractions. So maybe sitting at the kitchen or dining room table is a good starter. And don't have the TV on while they're trying to work, blaring out the theme tune to their favourite programmes. Do your best to create a quiet, helpful environment that'll work for them rather than against them. For instance, if you have your own work to do, try doing it at the same time. When they've finished, get them to show you what they've done. This will give you the chance to ensure they've completed what they were set. And above all, remember always to give praise where praise is due.

If your child isn't yet being given homework, you can neverthe-less help to instil these important principles in them ahead of time by getting them to spend half an hour every night reading. But don't overdo it: the more you can help your child see school as exciting and fun, the more interesting they'll find it and the more motivated they'll be to work hard later on. On the other hand, if it becomes a chore, they'll always struggle to get the job done.

 Top Tip: *By structuring your child's homework times **now**, you will help them to work well on their own later on.*

$e = mc^2$

If your child is having problems understanding things in the classroom or coping with their homework, talk to their teacher about it now. Don't put it off. Besides giving you a clearer indication about how they're doing in general, which is always helpful, it'll flag up to the teacher that more supervision is needed. And you may find that there's a simple solution to the problem, or at least that they've got some ideas about what you can do to help.

If your child seems to be having trouble in more than one subject, talk to their form tutor or year head to see if there's any discernible pattern. They may be struggling to keep up because they're not being taught at a pace and level that suits their ability. But the root of their problem could also be something as simple as bad eyesight, poor hearing or a common reading disorder like dyslexia. You may need to work alongside your child on their homework for a while, helping them gain confidence in a subject, for example, or improve their powers of concentration. You may even be able to get extra help for your child from the school.

But whatever you do, resist the temptation to start doing their homework *for* them. Success has a pretty hollow ring to it if you know that it was really your mum or dad who got top marks, not you! It might seem to help in the short term, but it's nothing short of a recipe for disaster in the long run. Rather than learning how to solve problems themselves, your child will become reliant on you. And, of course, you can't go into the exam room with them!

In the end, your action will cheat your child out of the pleasure of solving problems and learning what they can do if they put their mind to it. Instead, all they'll learn will be to give up whenever they hit difficulties, and they won't get the chance to build up a realistic picture of their strengths and weaknesses. You've got to help them learn to do things for themselves. Deep down they know this, of course, though they'll probably reserve the right to hate you for it in the meantime!

 Top Tip: *If your child is struggling in class or with their homework, talk to their teacher about it today.*

Chalk and Cheese

Sometimes problems in class or in a particular subject have nothing to do with your child's actual skills or abilities. For example, problems could be caused by something fairly easy to deal with, like their occasionally messing about or being distracted by the person they sit next to. Or the cause could be something more fundamental, such as problems with a particular teacher.

Each of our four children has had problems with their teachers at one time or another, either because of personality clashes or because for some reason a particular teacher wasn't able to give them the support or encouragement they needed. Sometimes it's because they got off on the wrong foot to begin with and never recovered. Sometimes it's just been a matter of 'chalk and cheese', where a teacher has failed to inspire our children because they've had such

71

different characters and interests. And on one or two rare occasions, we've found out as we've compared notes with other parents that the problem was the teacher themselves.

My friend Ellen always had trouble reciting her 'times tables'. For three years she was the only one in her primary class who couldn't stand up and rattle each one off in turn. Her seeming incompetence led to tension with her teacher, who even began to suspect that Ellen – an otherwise very bright student – was being deliberately useless! But though there was no love lost between them, the truth was that Ellen simply couldn't learn parrot-fashion. When she was finally put into a different class with a different teacher, her marks improved dramatically. Her new teacher concentrated on helping her improve at all the things she was naturally good at. At the same time, he taught her to calculate her tables from scratch without needing to memorise them. It took longer, but it meant she could approach a problem knowing she'd solve it eventually. For the first time, she says, she began to think that maths *wasn't* entirely beyond her reach. And she was right: today Ellen is a professor of applied mathematics at one of America's most prestigious universities.

If your child is struggling with a subject, start by talking to their teacher, even if you think they may be part of the problem. Be polite. Remember: there are always two sides to every dispute. See what you can do to help your child improve, and ask if there's anything they can recommend. If you're still not satisfied, talk to their form tutor or year head, or even the head teacher. As a very *last resort*, if your child seems to be struggling across the board and the school seems powerless to help, investigate the possibility of changing schools to one that seems more suitable to their gifts and personality.

Whatever you do, don't give up. Be persistent. After all, the school is there to support *you* in raising your child, not the other way around!

 Top Tip: *If you think the problem may be your child's teacher, talk to their head of year. Don't give up until you're satisfied.*

Pick on Someone Your Own Size!

What Should I Do if My Child's Being Bullied?

A few years back, the dance band D:ream had a song in the charts called 'Things Can Only Get Better'. Hugely popular, it became a kind of anthem for everyone from school sports teams to the Labour Party. But the truth is, things don't *always* get better. If problems are just swept under the carpet instead of being confronted and dealt with, they have a terrible habit of getting a whole lot worse.

If your child is being bullied, by far the *worst* course of action you could take is to ignore the problem altogether, hoping that it'll go away. This kind of 'head in the sand' manoeuvre is a guaranteed recipe for disaster. If you even suspect that your son or daughter is being picked on, it's vitally important for you to face the problem head on and try to find ways to help them deal with it. Otherwise, not only will it make them feel very insecure, but they'll carry these feelings with them into adulthood.

More than a quarter of all children are bullied at school or after school. Some studies even put the figure closer to a half. Being bullied inevitably makes children feel scared, and can turn their lives into a daily misery. And that's bound to have knock-on effects in terms of their school work and friendships. But the most damaging effect it'll have is in terms of their self-esteem. Bullying slowly erodes a child's self-confidence, sapping them of their belief in their own worth. It robs them of self-respect, giving them the impression that there's nothing about them worth respecting. So if you suspect that your child is being bullied, take action *today*.

 Top Tip: *If your child is being bullied, don't ignore the problem and hope it'll go away – it won't, so take action* **today**.

'Sticks and Stones ...'

Bullying takes many forms. It's often physical, but it can also be verbal and emotional. And contrary to the old adage, 'sticks and stones may break my bones but words will never hurt me', non-physical bullying can be very damaging indeed. Most children don't have the self-confidence to brush off continual verbal attacks. An insult or taunt may not be as obvious as a black eye, but its impact can last far longer. Bullying of any sort drains children of their self-confidence and reinforces their worst fears about themselves – however unfounded those fears may actually be.

Luke was always taunted at school. From an early age, other kids made comments about his weight. They were never vindictive, but they did make him self-conscious. He was already acutely aware that he was taller and broader than his friends, and this alone was enough to make him feel awkward, even if it was never commented on. As time went by, he slowly became more and more sensitive about his size and the constant put-downs, convinced there must be something very wrong with him. But his friends just assumed that, being big, he was tough enough to cope with the teasing. None of them could see the damage they were gradually doing to him.

When Luke moved up to secondary school, things got a lot worse. Some of the kids at the new school really started to take the mickey out of him. He hated it, but asking them to stop just made things worse. They sensed a weakness and exploited it. His school-work began to go downhill, which just gave the bullies more ammunition to use against him. When his parents saw how unhappy he was, they talked to his teachers. A few were sympathetic, but the head teacher said, 'This school doesn't have a real bullying problem. Luke's a big boy. He can handle it.' However, the truth was, Luke couldn't handle it. He stopped eating and started wetting the bed. He became more and more introverted, and began to do anything he could to get out of going to school. Today Luke has a serious eating disorder, and has tried to take his own life on several occasions.

Look out for the warning signs that your child is being bullied. The chances are that, if they *are* being picked on either physically or verbally, they will exhibit several classic 'symptoms', which can include:

- not wanting to go to school, especially for particular lessons or on particular days;
- developing sudden mystery illnesses such as headaches, tummy aches, etc.;
- losing schoolbooks or possessions, or having a number of them battered or broken;
- changing the route they take to get to school if you don't take them;
- coming home with unexplained bruises, scratches or torn items of clothing;
- becoming shy and introverted, or angry and unpredictable, at home;
- losing their appetite, having nightmares or trouble sleeping, or wetting the bed;
- getting consistently and inexplicably worse marks at school.

If you suspect your child is being bullied, don't wait for it to get worse – take action here and now.

 Top Tip: Bullying can be verbal or physical – look out for the telltale signs.

Confessions!

Being bullied isn't easy to talk about. In fact, any child faces a whole series of major obstacles in opening up about it to anyone. So if you think that your child is being bullied, resist the temptation to confront them about it too directly. Instead, try a more gentle, non-direct approach. First talk around the subject, giving them the opportunity to get used to it. Reassure them that they can trust you. And be patient. If they have been bullied, the longer it's been going on, the harder it'll be to talk about. Only ask them about it directly as a last resort.

When a child does begin to talk about being bullied, they'll be afraid of several things:

- **Being seen as weak.** Children often feel they should be able to sort out their own problems, which means that owning up to being bullied is the same as admitting to being a failure. It's crucial to help your child understand that being bullied doesn't mean they're weak, any more than being a bully would mean they're strong. (In fact, many bullies are themselves the victims of bullying.)

- **Being seen as the problem.** Most bullied children feel that they must have done something to deserve their fate. They're nervous about coming forward because they're worried that a parent or teacher will consider them just as much to blame as the bully. Let your child know that it's not their fault if they're being bullied. The blame always lies fairly and squarely with the bully.

- **Being seen as a 'grass'.** No child wants to get the reputation of being a telltale. They're afraid that, rather than stopping the bullying, it could be seen as a betrayal of their 'friends', leading to even bigger problems. Help your child to see that the real betrayer is always the bully, not whoever informs on him or her.

- **Not enough being done.** Perhaps the biggest reason that children who are being bullied don't come forward is the fear that not enough will be done to stop the bully. This creates a huge risk for a child. If the bully isn't sufficiently warned off to make them stop, the bullying is likely to get worse. In addition to all the previous 'reasons' for bullying, there'll be a new one! So your child needs to feel assured the bullying *will* stop if they report it.

- **Too much being done.** Victims want the bullying to stop, but they don't necessarily want the bully to get into a lot of trouble. They're afraid the bully's friends might take it badly, and then take it out on them, with the result that things end up going from bad to worse. What's more, a victim of bullying may feel responsible for what happens to the bully after they report them, which only adds to the misplaced guilt they already feel. Your child needs to be reassured that stopping the bullying is just as important for the bully as for the victim, and that though the punishment will fit the crime, it will go no further.

Top Tip: Give your child opportunities to talk about bullying, but try not to ask them directly if they're being bullied unless you really have to.

'That's YOUR Problem!'

As a hostage in Beirut in the 1980s, Brian Keenan was frequently locked in a room and chained to a wall or a radiator. There were no good reasons for him being held hostage. He'd done absolutely nothing to justify the cruel treatment he was being given. He'd just been in the wrong place at the wrong time, and fallen into the hands of men who were prepared to do anything to get what they wanted. In the end, he realised that his being a captive was nothing to do with him, and everything to do with his captors. In fact, in spite of the torture they were putting him through, he felt sorry for the men who'd taken him hostage. They acted like bullies because they felt powerless, and didn't know how to get what they wanted by normal means.

If your child is being bullied, they're probably trying to make sense of it by looking hard at themselves to see where the problem is. Especially if they're being called names, it's easy for them to assume that they're being bullied because there's something wrong with them. But the truth is, they're being bullied because there's something wrong with the person bullying them. So the more you can help your child to see bullying as a sign of weakness rather than strength, the more you can immunise them against its otherwise devastating effects.

My friend Paul has always been very short, but has a well developed sense of self-confidence. In fact, he's so short, he even had to stand on a stool to kiss his bride on their wedding day! At school, he was known as 'shorty', 'pint-size', 'small-fry', 'titch', etc. Even now, friends call him 'Small Paul'. But, he says, the comments about his size never really bothered him, because his parents – who're both on the short side themselves – had already done a good job of helping him develop a strong sense of self-esteem which immunised him against the taunts of the bullies at school. 'People would think it was really funny to call me "gnome" or something,' he recalls. 'But after you've heard it twenty-six times, it just gets boring. I used to ask them, "Is that the best you can do?" It was almost fun when they came up with something new. It meant they'd really had to think about it.'

 Top Tip: Help your child to see that bullying is a sign of weakness, not a sign of strength.

'Lead Us Not into Temptation ...'

Sometimes you can stop bullying from happening by taking some form of preventative action. For example:

- **Stay clear.** If the bullying often happens in a particular place – at the same spot in a playground or on the way home, for instance – then get your child to avoid that place in future. Teach them to play in a different part of the playground or take a different route home. Even if it means adding five minutes to the journey home, it'll be worth it if it means the bullying stops.
- **Stick together.** There's safety in numbers, even though a lot of bullies operate in groups themselves. Sticking with friends (even when going to the toilet, if that's where the bullying happens), can make a bully think twice. What's more, if the bullying does continue to happen, there are more witnesses who can describe what happened.
- **Walk away.** If the bullying happens on the way home, and you can't get anyone to go with them, teach your child not to stop, but always to walk away.

- **Travel empty-handed.** If they're being bullied for sweets, money or valuables, teach your child to do without for a while. Give them sweets at home rather than at school, and try to eliminate the need for them to carry money around with them. Give them cheap stationery and 'unexciting' pack lunches, and get them to leave their valuables at home. Once the bully realises there's nothing to be gained, they may lose interest.

- **Be assertive.** Teach your child to be assertive, holding their head up confidently and looking the bully in the eye. Help them to practise saying things like 'clear off' in the mirror beforehand. But whatever you do, don't encourage them to hit back. It'll probably do more harm than good.

 Top Tip: See if there's anything practical that your child can do to **avoid** being bullied.

Taking Action

A couple of years ago, I was hosting a television phone-in about bullying and a mum called to say that she'd been angry and concerned when she first found out that her son, Chris, was being bullied at school. She talked to his teachers, but despite their best efforts the bullying continued. Eventually she decided that the time had come for action. She marched down to the school, confronted the bully and – invited him to dinner! He was so startled by the invitation that the only thing he could think to do was accept.

Chris' mum figured that if the bully, Martin, could see what he was doing to Chris, he'd think twice before picking on him again. Things were awkward at first, but after a while she felt the conversation was getting somewhere. Martin revealed that he himself was often bullied by his brothers. His parents let it happen. Picking on Chris was just a way of venting his frustrations. The bullying stopped immediately, and Martin and Chris gradually became friends.

But not every story of bullying has this kind of happy ending, and not every bully is so easily won over. Sometimes all the self-confidence boosting and route-changing in the world won't stop someone from bullying your child. Firmer action needs to be taken.

If you find that your child *is* being bullied, you should *never* keep the information to yourself. Let their school know what's going on, especially if the bullying is happening during the school day (most bullying takes place at break times in the playground). The chances are that your child isn't the only one being bullied. So by making the school aware of the situation, you could be helping someone else's child as well as your own.

- Start by making a log of any instances of bullying you become aware of: verbal or physical. Write down the day, time and place of the bullying, as well as who was involved. This will help you and the school to get a good idea of the scale of the problem, as well as giving you some indication as to whether or not there's any pattern to it. It'll also help the school to find witnesses if it comes down to a case of your child's word against the bully's.

- When you approach their school, start by talking to your child's form teacher, or perhaps the teacher they get on best with. They may not have noticed the bullying, as it rarely goes on in plain sight and they have lots of pupils to deal with, but informing them about the situation will alert them to keep an eye open.

- If the school has a designated teacher to deal with bullying, talk to them as well. They can tell you what the school's policy on bullying is, and together you can talk about the best way to proceed. It's in the school's interest to stamp out bullying, so you should have a sympathetic ally. But don't expect the situation necessarily to improve overnight: bullying is often *learnt* behaviour, and it can take time for a child to *un*learn it. If a month or so drags by and nothing improves, however, speak to the head teacher. And if you receive no joy there, write to the school governors. Above all, don't give up.

- Sometimes even the school's best efforts will be thwarted by the attitudes of the bully's parents, who may not be willing or able to stop their child's behaviour. If this is the case you may need to consider taking legal action against the bully's parents (or against the school if they're not taking the problem seriously enough). A solicitor's letter may well be enough to spur them into taking action or seeking help.

Whatever you do, don't allow the bullying to go on. It's not only a violation of your child's rights – serious enough to be detailed in Article 19 of the United Nations Convention on the Rights of the Child – it's also a recipe for disaster.

 Top Tip: *Don't let your child suffer in silence – talk to their school.*

PART THREE: FRIENDS

Sex, Drugs and Alcohol

How Do I Talk about the Tough Issues?

Once, on a live phone-in show, a mum tearfully explained to me how her seventeen-year-old was totally out of control. Drink, drugs, violent and abusive behaviour – you name it, her child was into it. At the end of her tether, she sobbed, 'What can I do?' The tragedy was that, to a large extent, there was little she *could* do now except a bit of damage limitation. It was mostly too late.

It's like someone who's smoked sixty cigarettes every day of their adult life, and who's just been diagnosed as suffering from terminal lung cancer, phoning the doctor to ask what can be done to cure them. By that stage, sadly, the doctor can't cure them. The best that can be done is to help ease the pain.

Parents around the world worry about how they're going to cope with 'the teenage years' when the time comes. But the truth is that the key to defusing the 'teenage time-bomb' is to deal with it five or ten years before it's due to go off. The longer you leave it, the harder it gets, so it's wise to make your move early. Avoid a crisis at thirteen, fourteen or fifteen by starting work on your child's problems or potential pitfalls *now*, when they're still only seven, eight or nine years old. Don't put it off until it's too late.

Top Tip: *The longer you put off tackling tough issues like sex, drugs and alcohol, the harder it gets – so start* **now**!

Be Prepared!

It's one of life's most basic yet profound principles that preparation is the best form of protection. Firefighters and soldiers, for example, spend a lot of time practising for 'the real thing', because they know that the more prepared they are, the less likely they are to be hurt. Sent into dangerous situations, where their lives are constantly on the line, they rely on their training to help them achieve their goal without being killed or injured in the process. They're taught what to expect, and carefully rehearse ways to cope with whatever they might encounter. Adequate preparation can literally make the difference between life and death, and no modern army or fire brigade would dream of sending untrained recruits into the thick of things. But preparation is just as vital when it comes to helping your child cope with their sexuality.

In the Middle Ages, some fathers resorted to locking up their daughters in chastity belts as a guaranteed method of ensuring their purity. And out of love, concern and even fear for our children, it's sometimes easy to wish we could do the same kind of thing today. But the truth is, it wouldn't work. Even in medieval days, enterprising manacled daughters ended up bedding the handsome young blacksmith's apprentice in order to get a spare key cut. Nowadays they'd simply buy a Junior Hacksaw, learn how to pick the lock, or report you to Social Services!

So a wise parent makes it their aim to equip their child with a kind of *internal* chastity belt. In other words, they do their best to instil in them the only thing that can ultimately help and guide them – self-control.

We all know water can be dangerous, for example, and every parent keeps a watchful eye out when they take their young child anywhere near a lake, river or swimming pool in case they fall in. But what's the best way of preparing them for this? Should we keep them permanently away from water? Or teach them to swim? The clear choice, picked by millions, is of course swimming lessons. Preparation is vital. Why do some parents, then, abandon this wise approach and opt for an ivory tower when it comes to helping their child deal with tough things like sex, drugs and alcohol?

 Top Tip: *Preparation is better than cure, so protect your child from the problems of tomorrow by educating them today.*

It's Good to Talk ...

Even the most free-wheeling and permissive parents tend to become relatively traditional when it comes to their child and sex. It's natural for us to want to protect our children in every area of their lives, and this is doubly true in the arena of sex. Sexual decisions are the most intimate we can make. And sexual mistakes are often the most painful. In fact, it's no exaggeration to say that they can even be lethal.

But teenage sexuality is just as much a minefield for parents as it is for children. We want to trust our child eventually to make their own decisions. But we also want to keep them safe from harm. And we find it hard to adjust to the fact that the five-year-old we used to help dress will, in not that many years' time, become a sexually mature fifteen-year-old who inhabits an increasingly private world filled with their own choices.

So how *do* we provide them with that 'internal chastity belt'? How do we prepare our child for the inevitable? Part of the answer is simply to talk to them about sex – a prospect that sends shivers down every parent's spine. Don't worry, you're not odd. No parent ever talked to their child about sexuality without finding it a struggle at first just to get the words out – which, of course, is why so many parents put the whole thing off until it's too late. But however shy and embarrassed we are, the reality is that our children *need* to hear about sex from us. What's more, poll after poll shows that children *want* to learn about sex from us before they hear it from friends, magazines, the TV or even their school.

I learnt the facts of life from my mate John Dean one wet playtime when I was ten. These days, no child over the age of seven or eight can escape constant talk of sex. But the problem is that, without your involvement, what your child will pick up at this age is bound to be a worrying mixture of half-truths and misunderstandings. If you don't teach them about sex properly, they'll go on believing these myths well into the teenage years – with potentially disastrous consequences.

Some parents are worried that telling their child about sex will push them into sexual relationships earlier than they would otherwise, 'shattering their innocence'. But all the evidence suggests that just the opposite is true. As the saying goes, 'forewarned is forearmed'. Being armed with information usually delays a child's sexual activity. The truth is that *innocence* is more likely to be protected when *ignorance* is removed. Most of the eight thousand under-sixteens who get pregnant every year in the UK aren't even looking to have sex, let alone a baby! According to the Family Planning Association, most of them just get 'carried away'. In other words, they have sex without ever really deciding to. And the main reason why young people allow themselves to be swept along in the heat of passion? 'I just didn't know how to say No.'

Your openness and honesty will help your child to make better, more informed, more mature and more responsible choices when the time comes. Coping with hormones will be hard enough, but doing so without any guidance from you will be even tougher.

 Top Tip: *Ignorance is **never** bliss – it's potential disaster!*

One Step at a Time

Just this morning, I talked to a young mum who was about four months pregnant. Her three-year-old daughter had asked her why she was getting bigger. 'What do I tell her?' the woman asked. That's a question most parents want answered, and it doesn't get any easier when your child is eight or nine instead of three.

It's one thing to say 'start early', but what should we actually tell our child about sex? The first thing to say is that there's no easy-to-use, pre-prepared formula. Every child is different. But the best way to tackle the subject is to listen to their questions and comments, and deal with the issues as they crop up naturally in conversation. Rather than brushing questions aside or trying to avoid them altogether, answer them as openly and honestly as you can when they arise. The big advantage of this approach is that, as your child gets older and able to understand more, they'll be *used* to talking to you about sex and asking you awkward questions, so they won't be as shy about gradually making their enquiries more and more detailed. What's more, *you'll* be used to talking to them about sex, so it'll be easier and less embarrassing for you too – you won't get so hot under the collar about it.

Above all, don't save it up for the mother of all sex talks in which you sit your child down for a sombre and formal two-hour session, taking them slavishly through a book about sex or your own carefully written out notes (in case you forget anything). Nothing could make an already awkward situation worse. Instead, try to relate what you're saying to their life. Let them ask questions, and do your best to answer them. And if you *do* use a book – there's no reason why you shouldn't – use it to *start* a discussion, not avoid the need for one!

Of course, it'll still be embarrassing. In fact, you'll probably wish you could put a paper bag over your head to hide just how embarrassed you're feeling. But isn't embarrassment better than leaving the responsibility for teaching your child about one of the most important aspects of their life to a chance conversation with someone else in the playground? If *you* get it right when they're young, *they're* far more likely to get it right when they're older.

Top Tip: *Let your child raise the issue of sex and sexuality, but don't avoid it when they do!*

The Children's Edition Pop-Up Kamasutra

Whatever you do, be honest. Stories about storks, gooseberry bushes, or the birds and the bees may end an embarrassing moment quickly for you, but in the long run they'll just breed confusion, a lack of trust and potential embarrassment for your child.

When Sam arrived home from school, he was far from pleased. Summoning his parents to the living room, he announced in a loud voice, 'OK, let everyone in this house please stand advised that I, Samuel James Clarkson, have this day made a complete and utter fool of myself in sex education classes by repeating stories concerning storks told to me by certain parties residing herein!' If you insist on taking this kind of approach, when they eventually find out the truth about sex, your child will either begin to wonder either how many 'little white lies' you were prepared to tell them in order to end your embarrassment, or how anyone so sexually ignorant as you appear to be could ever have become a parent in the first place!

At the same time, don't feel you need to tell your child all the graphic details. Blow-by-blow descriptions of sex can make even less sense to a child than tales about storks. Too much information can be overwhelming and impossible to understand. When John asked his mum, 'Where did I come from?', she knew the time had finally come. Taking a deep breath, she launched into a full-colour, wide-screen, surround-sound, digitally enhanced biochemical explanation of egg, ovary, orgasm and intercourse. When she'd finished, half an hour later, John's only comment was, 'That's funny. Peter says he came from Brighton!'

You need to tell them the truth, but you don't need to tell them the *whole* truth *all at once*. Bit by bit will do fine. When Cornelia and I taught our kids how to tell the time, for example, we didn't sit them down and explain in great detail everything Einstein had to say about how time is relative to motion. (The main reason for this, of course, is that I don't have a clue myself!) Instead, we just told them about the big hand and the little hand and all the numbers in between. The rest could wait. We gradually told them more and more as they got older and were able to take it in.

In much the same way, you don't need to tell your child everything they'll ever need to know about sex when they first ask you where babies come from. Instead, slowly tell them more and more over several years. Give them as much information as seems appropriate at the time, never misleading or confusing them, but also never feeling it's your task to impart to your nine-year-old the entire contents of the Kamasutra!

Top Tip: Tell your child about sex on a gradual basis. Don't save it all up for the 'Big Talk'.

The Whole Story

However, it's vital for you to make sure that you don't confine your explanations about sex to the mechanics. Your task is to make sure that they understand more than simply what goes where, and when. And though it's crucial for your child to understand the potential perils and pitfalls of sex – sexually transmitted diseases, AIDS and unwanted pregnancy – and how the various forms of contraception available can help prevent these, if you've only told them about the physical aspects of sex, you've only given them half the story. They deserve for you to be honest with them about the morality as well as the mechanics of sex.

Your son or daughter will start thinking about girlfriends or boyfriends long before they start thinking about actually having sex. So learning how to cope with all the emotional hassles that accompany love will be essential if they're going to make wise sexual decisions later on. It's your responsibility to make sure they understand the moral and emotional aspects of sex and sexuality as well as the physical ones. Help them see how sex relates to the whole of their life, and how it fits into the framework of an on-going loving relationship. Don't leave them guessing: give them practical guidelines about *when*, *where* and *with whom* to have sex – not just *how*.

We all know that young people are often very insecure about themselves and their own worth, but recent research has shown that the more stable, secure and self-confident teenagers are, the less promiscuous they're likely to be. So the more you do to boost your child's self-confidence and self-esteem *now* – which includes giving them a good understanding of how sex and sexuality relates to them – the better equipped they'll be to make wise sexual choices in the years to come – and the longer that time will be in coming.

Top Tip: *Don't leave your child in the dark about how sex and relationships fit together – teach them the morals as well as the mechanics of sex.*

'All My Body Needs'?

The same basic approach – little, early and often – applies to talking with your child about the dangers of drugs. It's no good putting it off in the naïve hope that for some reason they'll never be faced with the temptation. By the time they leave school, most children will have been offered some kind of drug at least once and quite a few of them will have tried it. In fact, about 10 per cent of all twelve- to sixteen-year-olds and a third of all young people under twenty have tried an illegal drug. As ever, the best protection is preparation: the less you prepare them, the more defenceless they'll be.

The first drug of choice is usually the 'acceptable' one: tobacco. Whether swiped from a parent's handbag or bought from a vending machine, cigarettes are easily available and seem to offer children as young as seven or eight a one-stop-shop to instant adulthood. But the lessons your son or daughter learns about tobacco as a child could potentially influence their decision-making about hard drugs as a teenager. So it's vitally important to get it right now. If you don't want your child to smoke cigarettes or end up taking harder drugs – such as cannabis, Ecstasy or, at the top end, heroin or cocaine – then education will be vital.

All drugs, whether medicinal or illegal, are designed to tinker with the body's basic biochemistry. In the case of medicines, this is to correct an imbalance; with illegal drugs it's to create one. The upsides are often immediately obvious: tobacco calms you down, cocaine peps you up, cannabis makes you feel happier, Ecstasy boosts your energy levels and makes you high, heroin deadens your sensitivity to pain, LSD alters your perception of reality, etc. But there are also some deadly downsides: heroin and cocaine are highly addictive, and prolonged use is very bad for your health; cannabis is less addictive, but one or two joints can do as much damage to your lungs as ten or twenty cigarettes; and whilst the lethal effects of cigarettes are well known – lung cancer, throat cancer, heart disease, bronchitis, emphysema and gangrene – the long-term effects of Ecstasy on the brain are a complete mystery.

It's important to get your information right (and the section on further information at the back of this book can help you find out what you need to know), especially when it comes to understanding the distinctions between so-called 'hard' and 'soft' drugs. Your child will eventually come across a lot of 'misinformation' about drugs, so it's vital that your advice is correct and reliable.

 Top Tip: *No child is immune from being offered drugs, so education is vital.*

Just Say 'No'

But as with sex education, a knowledge of the facts isn't enough by itself. For example, children don't take up smoking because they're under the illusion there's nothing wrong with it (though it's true that they're *not* generally aware of the sheer enormity of the health risks). Most children start smoking because their friends are doing it. It's the adult thing to do, the 'sexy' thing to do. Most kids have even 'rehearsed' their first puff on a cigarette, miming the action from an early age. And even though they choke or throw up after inhaling the smoke, every child knows that persistence and conformity are the key if they're going to appear 'cool' and mature in front of their friends.

So if you don't help your child develop the self-confidence to say 'No' when they're offered cigarettes or other drugs, all the education in the world will be useless. They've got to feel good enough about themselves to stick up for their convictions, even if it means losing one or two so-called 'friends' in the process. They've got to build up the strength of character to know that they don't have to do what their friends are doing in order to be liked. Children who know they're loved unconditionally, and how valuable they are, are not only less sexually promiscuous, they're also more able to resist the peer pressure to smoke or take drugs. They're able to be themselves instead.

Of course, all of this confidence-building takes time. And the time to start is NOW!

Top Tip: *The self-confidence to say 'No' to drugs comes from knowing you're loved unconditionally.*

On the Bottle

When it comes to alcohol, the same lessons apply. You can pretty much guarantee that your child will have had a drink or two before the age of eighteen, and after that they're legally entitled to drink whatever they like. You can't keep your child away from alcohol for ever, so it's much better to prepare them for what's to come.

We know about 'alcoholism' and the perils of drink-driving, but while drinking too much will destroy your liver, there's strong evidence that a glass of red wine a few times a week is actually good for you! So preaching to your child about the dangers of the 'demon drink', especially if you're prone to having the odd glass or two yourself, isn't likely to do much good. In fact, the example you set could be crucial. If you handle your alcohol well, you'll be providing them with a responsible model to follow in learning how to drink wisely.

The chances are that your child *won't* grow up to be a teetotaller (even if *you* are). So it's important to teach them to treat alcohol responsibly: the answer to *ab*use isn't *non*-use but *right* use. As with sex and drugs, this will require an ongoing education – talking to your child about the pleasures and pains of alcohol when it crops up in the conversation. And because there's a lot of pressure on teenagers to have a drink with their friends, even when it's illegal to do so, you'll also have to build up your child's self-esteem and self-confidence before the teenage years if they're to stand any chance of doing what *they* want, not what their *friends* think they should be doing.

But with alcohol there's an extra option. In 1796, when smallpox was a deadly killer, the scientist Edward Jenner injected a young boy with tiny quantities of a weakened strain of the pox virus. He was convinced that he'd naturally produce the 'antibodies' he needed to fight it, and that these antibodies would make him immune to the full-strength virus when he came into contact with it. This process of inoculating people against a virus by giving them a weakened version of the real thing – known as 'vaccination' – is common practice today. But it can also work with alcohol.

James was allowed the odd sip of wine or beer at mealtimes from the age of ten, and a glass of his own at special occasions like Christmas or birthdays from the age of about fourteen. His parents wanted him realise that alcohol was a natural part of everyday life, not a 'big deal' or an exclusively 'adult' thing. They knew he'd be under considerable pressure to drink with his friends as a teenager, and they wanted him to learn how to handle it ahead of time. In addition, they wanted to take away the opportunity for him to see drinking as a form of teenage rebellion – if they let him drink at home anyway, there was nothing to rebel against. As a result, James says that when he left home to go to university, he was a lot more responsible than many of his new friends when it came to booze. 'You could always tell the people whose parents hadn't prepared them for alcohol,' he adds. 'They never knew when to stop.'

Top Tip: Preparation is always better than **prohibition**, so teach your child to handle alcohol wisely.

'One Day, Son, All This Will Be Yours ...'

How Do I Pass On My Values to My Child?

Until the mid-eighteenth century, sailing around the world was extremely hazardous. Sensible globe-trotting mariners would sail along a country's coastline whenever they could rather than risk the open sea, because there was no way to tell accurately where you were once you'd left the safety of land. But all that changed in 1759, when the clockmaker John Harrison invented the 'maritime chronometer'. With a chronometer, it was possible for the first time to pinpoint your exact position wherever you were in the world by comparing it to the famous Greenwich Meridian, which acted as a reference point. And that meant that you wouldn't get lost any more.

You can't hide your child from life's storms. They have to face them sooner or later, like everyone else. The only real question is how well equipped they'll be to cope when it happens – and that's up to you. Parents who pass on their values to their children are helping them develop a kind of 'moral chronometer'. Wherever they go and whatever they do in life, they'll be able to trust their judgment and make good moral decisions by using the values they learnt from you as a reliable reference point – a moral meridian.

 Top Tip: Without your values, your child will be all at sea!

New Brain-O – Washes Brains Whiter than White!

We've all heard about identical twins, separated at birth, who've got the same taste in food, clothes, music – even the opposite sex. Our genes play a vital role in determining the kind of person we turn out to be. But it's undoubtedly true that our character is also shaped by our influences, our choices and our upbringing, which is why we've also heard of identical twins, separated at birth, who turn out to have completely different tastes in music, fashion, friends and just about everything else. In other words, 'nature' and 'nurture' *both* play a part in deciding who we are and what we're like as people.

Now you can't do anything about your child's genes. He or she got them from you and is stuck with them (which is a good reason for being tolerant of their shortcomings). But you *can* do lots to influence their personality by giving them your moral values.

Some parents are worried about imposing their values on their children. They're afraid of over-influencing or even brainwashing them. But the truth is that everyone else is interested in influencing your child's values even if you're not. They're bombarded by different opinions on all sorts of subjects: sex, drugs, music, politics, the environment, money, fashion, faith, war, animal rights, homosexuality, careers, food, art, transport, race, gender, language, sport – the list is endless. Some of these are just opinions. But some are deliberate attempts to persuade your child that a particular view is the one they *should* have. Rightly or wrongly, there's a real battle going on for your child's mind (and money). So the question isn't, 'Is your child being brainwashed?' It's, 'What's your child's brain being washed with?'

When my friend Carey was a young girl, her father accepted a job in South Africa, which meant that the whole family had to move to Johannesburg. Her mum and dad had been brought up to believe that racism was wrong, so they tried to teach Carey and her brother that a person's skin colour doesn't make them better or worse than anyone else. But they were dismayed to find that their efforts were being continually undermined by many of their children's friends and teachers. In fact, they were both slowly picking up not only the accent of the white South Africans around them, but their pro-apartheid attitudes too. In the end, her dad became so worried about how Carey and her brother were turning out that he resigned his job and brought the family back to Britain.

The truth is, children are like sponges: they'll soak up their values from somewhere. So even if *you* don't influence them, someone else *will*. In fact, if you're not influencing your child, you're about the only person in their life who isn't. Someone else is doing it for you, only with *their* values and *their* standards, not *yours*. If your child is going to be influenced by anyone, don't you think it should be you? If you're not sure that your values are worth passing on, change them *now*! Because if they're not worth passing on, they're not worth having.

Top Tip: *If you're not influencing your child, you're about the only person in their life who isn't.*

Shrink-Wrapped and Sealed for Freshness?

The experts tell us that the average dad spends just three minutes a day in 'quality' conversation with their kids. The average mum does slightly better, knocking up five and a half minutes. By contrast, the average child spends three hours a day watching TV. So it doesn't take Einstein to work out who has the major influence on many kids' lives. Their values, morals, and beliefs are all shaped by what they see on TV. They're also constantly being influenced by school, music, magazines, computers, radio, books, advertising, videos, other adults, pressure groups, friends and friends' parents. In fact, your child is exposed to an overwhelming barrage of views and values every single day.

Of course, you can and should restrict the influences your child is exposed to. It's part of a parent's responsibility carefully to monitor what their kids watch on TV, see at the cinema or read in books and magazines, as well as where they go with their friends, etc. But none of this can ever produce a totally 'bad-influence-free' environment for them to live in. Whatever you do, you can't prohibit your child from being influenced by all sorts of views and opinions, however hard you try. So your *real* job is to prepare them by helping them understand and cope with these conflicting opinions better. And the best way of doing that is to talk to them about the issues, rather than pretending they haven't been raised.

The Eighteenth Amendment to the United States Constitution – which prohibited 'the manufacture, sale, or transportation of intoxicating liquors' – became law in 1920 and ushered in a thirteen-year period known as 'Prohibition'. It was a real attempt to address the serious problem of alcoholism in American society, but it was a total disaster. Not only did it fail to stop people drinking, it spawned ruthless gangsters like Chicago's Al Capone. By banning the 'demon drink', the government had hoped to save people from falling 'under the influence' of alcohol, but in fact all it did was to push the problem underground, where they had less control over it than ever. By the time Prohibition was repealed in 1933, most people had come to see that helping people to make mature and informed decisions ('preparation') was a far more effective policy than making those decisions for them ('prohibition').

Your child is at the beginning of their life. It's as though they're just setting sail on a lifelong voyage. But as yet their rudder doesn't guide them too well. They don't know how to make mature and sensible decisions, or how to understand all the opinions that bombard them. So it's your job to help them steer. It's your responsibility to stand at the helm with them, guiding and advising them as they turn the rudder. And this isn't just a duty, it's also a wonderful and extremely exciting privilege. So try not to miss out on it!

Top Tip: *You can't always protect your child, but you can prepare them.*

Captive Audience

But how *do* you pass on the right values? Well, the first thing to say is that it doesn't happen overnight. You can't sit your child down for a mammoth, six-hour, 'Big Value' talk and hope it'll do the trick. It's a slow process, like filling a bath from a dripping tap. So start NOW!

During the first years of their life, your child actively *wants* to copy what you do and say. You're their hero, and they want to be just like you. Nothing matters more to them than what you think. They want to know what you think about everything from world peace to Teletubbies. This time will pass, but what they learn from you now will lay the foundations on which their personality and whole approach to life will be built later on. So make sure you pass on your values while you still have the chance.

Work hard to find opportunities when you can deliberately pass on your advice, wisdom, views, opinions and beliefs to your child. It would be tragic if, when they were grown up, they had no idea what you felt about life's most important issues. So make sure they know *why* you hold the values you do.

Sit down with them for a 'quiet chat' over breakfast, or dinner in a restaurant (it needn't be expensive). You don't always need to have thought through what you're going to talk about beforehand, though on one or two rare occasions it may be useful to have an informal kind of 'agenda'. Most of the time, just taking the opportunity to find out what's happening in your son or daughter's life will give you the chance casually to discuss the moral dilemmas it raises. That way they'll learn that morality isn't a text-book subject – it's something that influences the ordinary choices we make every day of our lives.

Find out what they think, and then let them know what you think, so they've got a 'meridian' to help them steer their own course. You could even play devil's advocate a bit, prompting them to think things through by exposing them to the opposite view. You can be sure that their values will eventually be challenged, so it's better for them to have thought them all through properly in the safety of the home than elsewhere.

But above all, be gentle. We often reject advice, not because it's no good, but simply because it's given in such a way that we feel got at. The instinctive response to any kind of attack is to hit back. The one thing we *don't* do is listen. But that's what you want your child to do if they're going to benefit from your help and advice. So choose a time when they feel relaxed and confident.

Family mealtimes can also be a great time to pass on your values in an informal way. The only things some families ever seem to do together are eat and watch television, and even eating is usually done in front of the TV, more like grazing. But switching the TV off and spending the mealtime talking to one another instead is a vital part of building the relationships between you. In fact, in many European countries, the food is often the least important ingredient of a family meal. The primary aim is to enjoy each other's company in a relaxed environment, spending time with one another. And by unplugging the TV and turning mealtimes into a real family event, you can also pass on to your child one of your most important values: you regard spending time with your family as a top priority.

Whatever you do, don't put it off. Start today. Or the next time you turn around, they'll be grown up and it'll be too late.

 Top Tip: *Find a relaxed place to pass on your values to your child, and talk about issues as they come up.*

Follow My Leader

Many of your values are passed on *accidentally*. From long before the time they're able to make 'value judgments', your child will copy what you say and do, both consciously and unconsciously. They'll adopt your gestures and mannerisms without even thinking about it. But they'll also swallow some of your values.

So if you don't want your child to learn something from you, don't do it. Whatever you tell them about your values, they'll check to see how it all works out in practice in your life. For instance, it's no use trying to teach them about honesty if you then ask them to lie and say you're not in to answer the phone when you are. The old adage, 'do as I say, not as I do', never works. If you try to teach your child values you don't actually live by, they'll know it. And they'll come to an obvious conclusion: you're a hypocrite. As a result, they'll probably reject your values, and maybe even you as well. So get your act up to scratch. If you want them to do it, make sure they see you doing it. And if you don't want them to do it, don't do it yourself!

Every parent is charged with the huge responsibility and the wonderful privilege and joy of being a role model and shaping a life – perhaps even moulding someone who'll one day become a parent themselves. In other words, the values your child catches from you may eventually be caught by *their* children, so you're not just shaping your child's life, but those of your grandchildren as well! All parents are role models. The only question is, what kind of role models are we? How good a job are we doing?

The way we parent our child is the single most crucial factor in determining who they become. One day, they'll look in the mirror and realise just how much like you they've turned out. If you're honest and kind, they're likely to be honest and kind. If you're rude and arrogant, they're likely to be rude and arrogant. If you're lazy, they may well end up just like you. And if you use violence and bullying to get your way, they could end up trying the same trick. You're in a very powerful position, so it's vitally important that you get it right.

Top Tip: *If you don't want you child to learn it from you, don't do it!*

The Heart of the Family

The truth is, secure families produce secure children. Families come in all shapes and sizes, and many of them, for one reason or another, have only one parent. However, if you have a partner, the quality of your relationship with them will have a huge impact on your child. Your relationship is the heart of your family. So if it's a continuous war zone, this will have a detrimental effect on your child.

If you and your partner are constantly rowing, for example, it's almost bound to affect your son or daughter's performance at school. It'll be almost impossible for them to keep their minds on their lessons or homework if they're worried about things falling apart at home. What's more, they're likely to feel partly to blame for everything, and anxiety and guilt don't motivate kids to do well at school. What they need to know is that, however tough the big world is, home is fun and secure.

When children see their parents fall out of love with each other, it's only natural for them to begin to wonder if they still love *them*. After all, if you stop loving each other, why shouldn't you stop loving them? Of course, most parents who go through a divorce or break-up couldn't stop loving their children if they tried. But this isn't at all obvious to the children involved. So it's vitally important that through all the loo-cleaning, kid-ferrying, clothes-washing, key-losing, meal-cooking, sink-unblocking, supermarket-shopping, cat-feeding, bill-paying, vomit-clearing, mundane tasks of everyday life, you work hard to keep the romance alive. And when it's not there, you continue working hard at loving each other through all the arguments and hard times. Don't be afraid to kiss or cuddle in front of your child. Knowing that you love each other helps reassure them that you love them, too.

 Top Tip: *Be romantic with your partner if you have one – secure relationships produce secure children.*

Should I Stay or Should I Go?

But what if things have reached the point where you and your partner are thinking about separation or divorce? Is it better to stay together for sake of your child or not?

For the last thirty years, the experts told us that staying together was always counter-productive because the children knew it was an empty sham. In an ideal world, they'd *want* you to stay together - what child, hand on heart, *wouldn't* want their mum and dad to love each other and be happy ever after? But, the argument went, children were far more robust than they were given credit for. They were mature enough to accept the fact that you couldn't stay together. What mattered most to them was that their mum and dad were both happy and free to be themselves, instead of feeling trapped.

But recent research has turned this view entirely on its head. The days of pretending that kids don't mind whether their parents decide to split or not are over. The fact is, all children function better in a secure and settled environment. Their schoolwork is better, their behaviour is better and they're less likely to leave home or dabble in under-age sex (often simply a misguided cry for attention and love). Except where there's domestic violence or abuse, children are happier when their loyalties aren't divided. They're more secure when they're not being ferried between different homes. So the view now is: if at all possible, *do* stay together for the sake of the children. They didn't ask to be born, so you owe it to them to put them first. It's nothing more than common sense, really.

Sometimes, of course, staying together isn't an option. Your marriage or relationship won't work, and all your attempts to *make* it work have failed. Sometimes you don't have a choice. Your partner has walked out on you and you're on your own. And on top of all your other worries, you're very concerned about how your child is coping.

If you separate, decide to get divorced or find yourself abandoned, what can you do to help your child adjust better to their new situation?

- Never blame them for the breakup of your relationship. It's not *their* fault if *you* can't get on with your former partner. This may be obvious to you, but it's far from obvious to them. Most kids feel responsible when their parents bust up. You must do all you can to allay their fears, because they'll turn into a deep sense of guilt without your reassurance. Don't wait for it to become an issue. Do all you can to get the message across. Assure them it's not their fault. Explain to them why they shouldn't feel guilty.

- Agree with your ex-partner beforehand what you're going to say to your child. Then sit down and talk to them *together*. Explain, as simply as you can, what's going on. If talking to them together isn't possible, at least try to agree on your story. Giving them two different versions will only leave them wondering whether they can believe either of you, and will probably lead to them inventing their own version of events.

- Tell them the truth, not half-truths. Gaps in their knowledge will quickly be filled by their imagination – or playground rumours.

- Divorce or separation is like bereavement. So whatever you say, expect your child to go through periods of shock, denial, resentment, anger, confusion and grief before slowly coming to terms with the situation.

- Tell them about all the practical problems, and answer all their questions as honestly as you can. They'll want to know where they are going to live and how much they'll see each of you. They'll feel very insecure and worried about big changes such as leaving their friends, school, etc.

Above all, don't use your child as a pawn in your own power game. You're divorcing each other, not them, so don't use them as weapons or try to get to your ex-partner through them. They need the love and support of *both* of you, so never moan about each other in their presence. Whatever you may think of your ex-partner and their behaviour, don't run them down in front of your child. They automatically love both of you, so if they hear you bad-mouthing your ex-partner, it won't help their respect for you either.

 Top Tip: If at all possible, **do** stay together for the sake of your child.

Single Life

When two parents are involved in raising a child, there's great comfort in the fact that you're not the only one on show. But for a single parent, things are different. Unless you've got a close friend or family member who can act like a kind of 'adopted' parent, the responsibility falls entirely on your shoulders. You're on show twenty-four hours a day, and there's usually no one to talk through the issues with.

In effect, you're permanently *on duty*, and that's a very demanding job. Even when you're sick, depressed or upset, you still have to run the home, maintain discipline and show your child you love them. And in the midst of the chores and responsibility, it can seem almost impossible to find quality time for your child – even for a meaningful chat, let alone for having fun together! To make matters even tougher, there's often an unkind stigma attached still to being a single parent. Some people frown on you because they seem to think that just being a single parent is a crime in itself.

The truth is, of course, that people become single parents for all sorts of reasons. Few would choose that pathway in an ideal world, and the vast majority do a fantastic job without the kind of support and backup that most two parent families count on. In fact, many single parents end up doing a far better job than many families where both parents are present.

But if you're a lone parent, be careful about who you let step into a position where they become a role model for your child. Because whoever you choose, they'll begin to impose *their* values on your children, whether they mean to or not. And because they're so much closer and more influential even than friends or the television, what they say will carry a lot of weight. So even if you feel under enormous pressure, make your choices carefully. At the end of the day, it's *your* values that your child will need as a meridian, helping them to navigate life's storms, not someone else's.

Top Tip: *If you're a single parent, choose your helpers carefully.*

Do the Right Thing

How Can I Help My Child Become a Responsible Person?

I remember the day Cornelia and I took our first child to nursery school. We were both a bit scared about leaving her there on her own. So as we arrived at the nursery gates, we were greatly relieved to see that there were plenty of other mums and dads there, also dropping their children off for their first day. And just like us, I could tell they were all subtly inspecting not only the chairs, desks, paint pots and crayons inside the classroom, but the playground outside as well. I could see them checking for sharp edges and hard surfaces, exactly like me, and being just as reassured as I was to find that the 'tarmac' was rubberized, the climbing frames weren't too high, and the boundary fence around it all was good and firm.

Like all parents, we wanted to know that our daughter would be safe from harm when she was at nursery. For four years, Emily had spent almost every waking moment with Corni. It was a big step for her and us to move up to the nursery. We wanted her to learn to be more independent than she could be at home, but we also wanted to ensure that she had this freedom within secure and sensible limits. The nursery provided a controlled environment: freedom within safety limits.

Boundaries are vital for all children, whatever their age. They all need the protection that clear limits offer them. And family rules act a bit like a nursery's controlled environment and firm boundary fence, marking the safe limits beyond which a child mustn't go, but within which they enjoy freedom. Everything inside the boundary is safe, but everything beyond it is strictly 'out of bounds'.

It's no good simply telling kids to 'act your age' when they get things wrong and behave badly. Most of the time they behave as they do precisely *because* they're acting their age! That's the point. And that's why they need rules: to protect them until they're old enough and experienced enough to make sensible decisions for themselves, as well as to give them an invaluable reference guide for learning to make these decisions.

The goal is slowly to enlarge this 'playpen', because as they grow and develop, they'll need and will be able to handle greater and greater levels of freedom and choice, which previous, tighter limits will have taught them to handle wisely. Over time, strict rules will gradually give way to trust. The idea is that by the time they're able to break down the perimeter fences altogether, they won't want to, because by then they'll appreciate and enjoy living in a way that both respects and protects others as well as themselves.

 Top Tip: You need to set rules that give your child freedom within safe limits.

Going to Extremes

Family rules, like a nation's laws, are there to give freedom within safe limits. They're not just a way of managing chaos. They're a vital part of every parent's responsibility to protect their kids from harm, and to teach them right from wrong.

Your child, like everyone else's, will inevitably push against the boundaries you set them, to see how far they can be stretched – and even whether they can be kicked down and trampled underfoot altogether! But at the same time, they actually rely on them being there for protection. So the boundaries you set, like the walls of a playpen, must provide your children with both *limits* and *freedom*, because they'll need *both* if they're to grow up to become constructive and responsible members of society.

Allowing a child to do what they like when they like is *not* the hallmark of a loving parent. In fact, it's just the opposite. Without well-drawn limits on behaviour, a child will grow confused and insecure. How can they be sure what's right and what's wrong?

In fact, no parent sets *no* limits. But in a home where they're not clearly defined and consistently maintained, the ones that *do* get enforced are often unpredictable and totally dependent on a parent's mood swings. The result is that a child never knows where they stand or what's expected of them. What's more, by not giving clear guidelines, parents only store up trouble for their child later on: having never learnt how to behave acceptably, they'll eventually come up against someone – at school, work or elsewere – who will step in to 'teach them a lesson they'll never forget'.

But if being too permissive is a mistake, then being too

117

authoritarian is just as short-sighted. If limits are set in stone with no discussion or understanding, and new limits are sometimes imposed without warning or explanation, then a child doesn't so much live in a playpen as a prison cell. This kind of jump-when-I-say-jump regime gives no room for mistakes, choices or growth. Rather than being kept safe, children are simply strait-jacketed. The problem is, your child will one day *do* what they want, *go* where they want, *wear* what they want, *say* what they want, and *see* who they want anyway. But they won't have had enough experience of freedom to know how to handle it wisely. In the long term, setting rigid and authoritarian limits is every bit as disastrous for your child as setting no limits at all.

So a sensible parent will steer a middle road, creating a flexible framework of rules, discipline and freedom that'll prepare and train their child to be able to make their own wise decisions in the future.

 Top Tip: Setting harsh limits is as disastrous as setting no limits at all.

A Stitch in Time ...

But being flexible doesn't mean making it all up on the spur of the moment. Forward planning is essential. Every football manager knows they can't predict the outcome of a game, let alone anticipate every possibility on the pitch ahead of time, but they still devise not only a plan of action for each game, but also an overall strategy for the whole season. It's flexible enough to leave room for manoeuvre, but it still has to be there.

In the same way, though you'll always have to do *some* improvising, you need to think ahead. It's impossible to anticipate every disciplinary problem that'll hit your home, and you're bound to have your fair share of crises, just like every other family. But the truth is that some families have far *more* than their fair share of crises. No sooner has one domestic catastrophe been dealt with than another explodes. As a result, the parents spend their whole time involved in 'crisis management', simply because they don't think and plan ahead. A little advanced planning can save you a great deal of hassle in the long run.

The key is to think about and develop your family rules – the safe limits you place on your child's behaviour – *before* you need them. Don't fool yourself that you won't need them, because sooner or later you *will*. Instead, take the time to think through the issues and talk to other parents you respect – ones who've been there before you – about their approach. If you don't plan ahead, establishing the limits firmly in your own mind and then telling your child about them and the issues that surround them, you'll probably end up making hot-headed decisions on the spur of the moment that you'll regret later.

What's more, you can't expect your child to do what you say unless you've told them in advance what that is. They're not a mind-reader, and they're unlikely to be able to guess. So try to stay one step ahead of your child, tackling problems before they even occur by ensuring they know exactly where they stand, stating clearly and ahead of time what the limits are. Talk about them with your child, helping them to understand why they exist in the first place.

A rule is never enough on its own. 'Do as I say and don't argue' is never the best policy. It's always best to back up your rules and limits with clear information and open discussion on why they need to be there. The more understanding a child has about why rules or limits exist, the more responsible their behaviour will tend to be (though you do need to remember they're still a child!), and the fewer rules you'll actually need to set.

 Top Tip: *Think about your house rules, and why they're needed, **before** you need them.*

The Ten Commandments

Having just a few rules about your child's behaviour is better than having lots of them. After all, even God only gave humanity ten commandments, not 250! The more rules you make, the more you have to remember – and enforce. Your rules should always be reasonable and necessary, but above all they need to be enforceable. So decide what really matters, and only make rules about these things. Keep them to a minimum.

For instance, there are four main rules in our house which cover virtually everything else. We've phrased these rules positively, not negatively:

1   Always tell the truth.
2   Always show other people courtesy, care and respect.

3 Always work together as a family and talk about problems.
4 Remember that trust needs to be earned.

These four 'Golden Rules' are the basis for other, more specific rules that change as time passes and generally have a built-in sell-by date: tidy your bedroom, don't hog the computer, go to bed at the right time, do your homework when you first get it, clean out the rabbit hutch on Saturday morning, etc.

When the founders of the United States of America drew up their written Constitution – the basis of all US law – they didn't write down every little rule that came into their heads. Instead, they worked out what they thought would be essential if the country was going to be run smoothly and fairly, and then wrote down seven 'articles' covering the basics. A few years later, they made ten Amendments, including the right to free speech and the right to 'bear arms'. But since its official adoption in 1789, the Constitution has been the 'gold standard' by which every law in the USA is measured. No town, district or state can pass a law that goes against the Constitution.

Why not draw up a sort of 'Constitution' for your family, like the four 'Golden Rules' we have for ours? It's better to have a few rules that are clearly understood by everyone than to have so many that you need to write them all down in a massive 'Law Book'. If you're constantly inventing new rules, your child will quickly become bewildered. But if they know in advance what your basic 'Constitution' is, you can always introduce new, specific rules by showing how they're a practical outworking of the original framework. In our house, for example, 'Don't hog the computer' is merely a way of ensuring that our children are courteous to each other and work together as a family.

Top Tip: *Devise a short 'Constitution' for your family, enshrining the values you think are the most important.*

Dos and Don'ts

From the Garden of Eden to Al Capone, prohibitions haven't worked too well. There's something about a firm command *not* to do something that makes us immediately want to go out and have a go at it! So whenever you can, try to phrase your rules as positive goals rather than a list of 'thou shalt nots'.

You'd be surprised how well this can work. When one of my sons finally found the courage to tell me he'd made a small hole in the dining room window by catapulting a stone through it earlier that day, he was shaking from head to foot. He was probably convinced that the world – or at least *his* world – was about to end. He knows that even *throwing* stones in the garden isn't allowed, let alone propelling them by catapult! But it showed great strength of character for him to tell me the truth when he didn't have to, so we weren't furious that he'd broken a small rule. He knew he'd made a bad mistake already. Instead, without letting him feel that his 'crime' didn't matter, we made sure he knew how proud we were that he'd owned up, keeping our first family rule: always tell the truth. That day, we reinforced three lessons:

1 Truth is more important than windows.
2 It always pays to tell the truth, however hard it is at the time.

3 Think about the possible consquences of an action before you take it.

The only alternative response, which I admit was rather tempting, was flying off the handle and shouting threats at him in a deafening voice. But whilst this might have made me feel better in the short term, in the long term it would just have taught him to cover his tracks better and learn how to lie more effectively!

When family rules are just a long list of *don'ts*, parents seem more like judges than friends. But if your child knows you value their honesty, and love them no matter what, they'll be more able to admit when they've done something wrong. What's more, they'll slowly feel able to come and talk to you about other things as well.

Don'ts are necessary, but they should never overshadow the *dos*. The more positive you can make your family rules, the more effective they'll be, because your child will come to see that the limits aren't there to spoil their fun, but to protect them and help them become independent, responsible people. By talking things through with them, you can begin to help them learn how to make safe and sensible choices. At the same time, you avoid the need for so many negative rules as they get older because they'll slowly learn to judge for themselves how their behaviour fits in with the family 'Constitution'.

But remember, your child will find it hard to agree to rules that don't make any sense to them. And even if they *do* agree, they'll resent them, and you for making them. As they get older and start to work things out for themselves, your child is more likely to break a rule because it doesn't make sense to them than because they're being naughty. If the rule is unreasonable, you'll only lose authority and respect by enforcing it. Even if it *is* reasonable, you could still lose authority and respect by not explaining it in a clear, calm and logical way. So try to explain the limits in such a way that they make sense to your child. The more they make sense, the more likely they are to be accepted.

The older your child gets, the more involved they can and *should* be in shaping family rules in the first place. They can even agree the punishments for breaking them. Though your family isn't a democracy – you're the boss! – by acting as if it *were* much of the time you can help train your child to take responsibility for their own life. If they feel they 'own' the rules, they'll be less likely to break them – and more inclined to accept the penalties when they do.

But watch out: the limits you set are likely to include checks on *your* behaviour as well as theirs! Like it or not, you undermine your own rules whenever you violate them or unreasonably claim they don't apply to you. It confuses kids when adults seem to play by a whole different set of rules. So if you make a rule that doesn't apply to you, try to explain *why* you're exempt. The more fair and reasonable your total package of rules is, of course, the easier this task will be.

 Top Tip: *The more positive your family rules are, the more effective they'll be.*

Following the Green Cross Code

Self-confidence and self-discipline develop as you're slowly willing to grant your child greater and greater levels of responsibility, and the freedom that goes with it. This is the best way a parent has of saying, 'I trust you'. If you don't do this, your child will never *feel* trusted or trustworthy. And that inevitably means they're unlikely to *become* trustworthy.

Peter and Janice recently told me about the first time they let their two daughters – aged seven and nine – walk to school on their own. The experiment was a total disaster. Janice had told them that she'd be following about twenty metres behind, just in case. And because they knew she was behind, and wouldn't let anything bad happen to them, they didn't take things seriously. In fact, they paid so little attention to road safety that it was a wonder they didn't get run over.

But rather than calling the whole experiment off, Janice told the girls they were now ready to go to school *entirely* on their own the next day. She followed them anyway, of course, but this time made sure they never even suspected she was there. The two girls couldn't have done better. Thinking they were alone, they acted quite differently. They held hands, walked sensibly, and stopped, looked and listened where they were *meant* to stop, look and listen. Entrusted with the task of looking after themselves, they behaved responsibly and with perfect care.

The art of delegation is the art of knowing when to move from a strict set of rules to ever greater degrees of trust and responsibility. And the better you know your child, the more able you are to make good judgments about how and when to do this. Too much responsibility too soon can be totally overwhelming, but too little will always leave them believing you don't trust them.

It's vital to understand that delegation is *not* about just washing your hands of responsibility. Some people see it as a way of passing the buck. But that's not delegation – it's dumping! In my job, I delegate huge amounts of work. But this doesn't mean I'm no longer responsible for it. Though the work is entrusted to others, it's my job to make sure that they're getting all the backup, support and guidance they need. If things are going badly, it's just as much my fault as anyone else's. Delegation is about *sharing* responsibility with others, not dumping it on them. *They* are responsible for the details, but I'm responsible for *them*. If they've been given too much responsibility to handle, or too little to inspire them, then I haven't delegated well.

So mums and dads still remain ultimately responsible for all the things they delegate to their child, and therefore for checking how they're getting on. Rather than blaming them and giving up when things are going wrong, they need to tweak the system a little bit by adjusting the level of responsibility given.

Delegation can be extremely frustrating. When you first teach someone to do something, there are bound to be 'teething problems'. Mistakes are inevitable when you're learning something new. At this point, every parent faces the temptation to take the reins back and do it themselves. But trusting someone with a task and then taking it away again is like saying that you've realised they're not trustworthy, and the end result will be worse than it was to start with.

 Top Tip: *Delegation is a way of telling your child you trust them.*

'Three, Two, One ...'

Getting the balance right, and slowly allowing your child to replace *your* rules with *their* judgment as they get older, is one of the most difficult challenges any parent faces. Some rules obviously come with built-in 'sell-by' dates. 'Don't cross the road on your own', for instance, won't be appropriate for ever.

Unfortunately there's no chart available setting out the precise schedule for the move from a strict set of rules to greater freedom and trust, and even if there were, it would be useless. Each child is unique: they handle responsibility in their own way and in their own time, which means that once again it's the time you invest in getting to know your child – its quantity and quality – that will be your best guide.

It's all a bit like teaching your child to ride a two-wheeler. You start by promising not to let go of the saddle, and run alongside as they get the feel of it. Then, when they're confident enough, you let go – just for a second or two. Eventually, when they're able to go short distances on their own, you let go for longer periods, still running alongside just in case. It's what every parent does. But even so, it's different every time because each child is unique. For example, our first daughter learnt to ride a two-wheeler in ten minutes flat, while our elder son took several weeks to achieve the same thing.

Just as with learning to ride a bike, there's no universal timescale for letting your kids go and giving them responsibility and freedom. Each child responds to love, freedom, discipline and instruction in different ways. Some need more guidance, others less. And this means that treating each child *fairly* isn't the same thing as treating them all *the same*. In our house, for instance, if we let our kids set their own bedtimes, the girls would always go to bed at a reasonable time. The boys, on the other hand, would never voluntarily enter their bedrooms. They'd wake up tired, late and stiff the next morning, still in their clothes in front of the TV in the living room. This has nothing to do with their ages, and everything to do with their characters.

The parent who's looking for a list of *do*s and *don't*s, and a firm timetable for letting go, is the kind of parent who'd make mistakes even if such timetables were available. In order to work out when to keep your child on a tight lead and when to let go, you need to spend time getting to know them well. There's no alternative and no short cut to this. You've got to make time to get to know their wants and needs, their strengths and weaknesses, and their unique ways of seeing the world. If you don't, you'll simply end up reacting to their behaviour in a non-constructive way rather than thoughtfully working to shape it with them.

So try to get to know your child even better, think about the appropriate level of responsibility to delegate to them, keep your cool when the problems inevitably occur, encourage them by pointing out what they did *right,* and urge them to try again when they fail. This way, they'll slowly grow in confidence, expertise and – because they feel *trusted – trustworthiness*. They'll grow into being responsible people.

 Top Tip: Spend time getting to know your child – it's the only way to know how much independence to give them.

THE LAST WORD

The Navajo Indians of North America incorporate a kind of 'Marriage Race' into every wedding, as I found out a few years ago when I went to one. As part of the ceremony, all the women in the village run around its boundaries with the new bride. The bride finishes this 'race' first, with her immediate family – her mother, aunts and sisters – close behind, and all the other women just behind them. This isn't a tradition designed to ensure that all the women of the village get regular exercise. It's a powerful symbol of the way the Navajo recognise that we all need ongoing support from the whole community.

There was a time when you'd have known just where to turn for help in our society too. Uncles, aunts, parents, grandparents and great-grandparents all lived in the same village. They were on hand to offer useful and relevant guidance, support and babysitting when you needed it. But the family has shrunk considerably in the last century. Fifty years ago, your mother lived in the same street. A hundred years ago, she lived in the same house. Now you're lucky if she even lives in the same part of the country. Smaller families have given us independence, but at what cost? As extended families grow apart, we're becoming more and more isolated. Entire communities used to play a part in raising every child. Now we often feel as though we're out on our own, left to fend for ourselves.

But the truth is, you're *not* alone. Beyond this book, there are all sorts of resources available in the difficult, but rewarding, task of being a parent. From books and videos to courses and specialist organisations, help is literally only a phone call away. The next few pages give just an example of the kind of resources on offer, but for more information you can write to **Parentalk** at:

PO Box 23142, London, SE1 0ZT

Whatever you do, *don't* try to go it alone. You can be a great parent, so if you need help, get in touch.

FURTHER INFORMATION

Organisations

Parentalk
PO Box 23142
London SE1 0ZT

Tel: 0171 450 9072/9073
Fax: 0171 450 9060
e-mail: pa.rentalk@virgin.net

Provides a range of resources and services designed to inspire parents to enjoy parenthood.

Positive Parenting Publications
1st floor
2A South Street
Gosport PO12 1ES

Tel: 01705 528787
Fax: 01705 501111
e-mail: info@parenting.org.uk
Web site: http://www.parenting.org.uk

Aims to prepare people for the role of parenting by helping parents, those about to become parents and also those who lead parenting groups.

Gingerbread
16-17 Clerkenwell Close
London EC1R 0AA
Tel: 0171 336 8183

Fax: 0171 336 8185
e-mail: office@gingerbread.org.uk
Web site: http://www.gingerbread.org.uk

Provides day-to-day support and practical help for lone parents.

Parent Network
Room 2
Winchester House
11 Cranmer Road
London SW9 6EJ

Tel: 0171 735 1214
Fax: 0171 735 4692

Provides support and education groups for parents in local communities.

Parentline
National Office
Endway House
The Endway
Hadleigh
Essex SS7 2AN

Tel: 01702 559900
Fax: 01702 554911
e-mail: parentline-uk@dial.pipex.com

Provides a confidential telephone helpline for anyone in a parenting role.

NSPCC
42 Curtain Road
London EC2A 3NH

Tel: 0171 825 2500
Fax: 0171 825 2525
e-mail: marcomm@nspcc.org.uk
Web site: http://www.nspcc.org.uk

*Aims to prevent child abuse and neglect
in all its forms and give practical help to
families with children at risk.*

**Stepfamily (National Stepfamily
Association)**
Chapel House
18 Hatton Place
London EC1N 8RU

Tel: 0171 209 2460
Fax: 0171 209 2461
e-mail: tnsa@ukonline.co.uk

*Provides support, advice and
information for stepfamilies and those
who work with them.*

Care for the Family
PO Box
Cardiff CF1 1RE

Tel: 01222 810800
Fax: 01222 814089
e-mail:
care.for.the.family@dial.pipex.com
Web site:
http://www.care-for-the-family.org.uk

*Providing support for families through
seminars, resources and special projects.*

Home-Start UK
2 Salisbury Road
Leicester LE1 7QR

Tel: 0116 2339955
Fax: 0116 2330232

*Committed to promoting the welfare of
families with at least one child under five.*

Kidscape
152 Buckingham Palace Road
London SW1W 9TR

Tel: 0171 730 3300
Fax: 0171 730 7081

*Works to prevent the abuse of children
through education programmes involving
parents and teachers, providing a range
of resources. Also runs a bullying
helpline.*

YouthNet UK
e-mail: youthnet@thesite.org.uk
Web site: http://www.thesite.org.uk

*Aims to give young people access via the
Internet to the most comprehensive
information available.*

National Drugs Helpline
0800 77 66 00
c/o Health Education Authority
Trevelyan House
30 Great Peter Street
London SW1P 2HW

*Free helpline offering confidential advice.
Can also send out free leaflets and
answer any questions callers might have.*

Publications

The Sixty Minute Father, Rob Parsons, Hodder and Stoughton
How to Succeed as a Parent, Steve Chalke, Hodder and Stoughton
Sex Matters, Steve Chalke and Nick Page, Hodder and Stoughton
Positive Parenting: Raising Children with Self-Esteem, E. Hartley-Brewer,
  Mandarin Paperback
Raising Boys, Steve Biddulph, Thorsons
The Secret of Happy Children, Steve Biddulph, Thorsons
Families and How to Survive Them, Skinner and Cleese, Vermilion
Stress Free Parenting, Dr David Haslam, Vermilion
How Not to be a Perfect Mother, Libby Purves, HarperCollins

Parenting Courses

- **Parentalk Parenting Course**
  A new parenting course designed to give parents the opportunity to share
  their experiences, learn from each other and discover some principles of
  parenting.

  Parentalk
  PO Box 23142
  London SE1 0ZT

- **Parent Network**
  Operates through self-help groups run by parents for parents known as
  Parent-Link. The groups are mostly run for 2 or more hours, over 13 weekly
  sessions. For more information phone 0171 735 1214.

- **Positive Parenting Publications**
  Publish a range of low cost, easy to read, common sense resource materials
  which provide help, information and advice. Responsible for running
  a range of parenting courses across the UK. For more information phone
  01705 528787.

The Paren talk Parenting Course

Helping you to be a Better Parent

Being a parent is not easy. **Parentalk** is a new, video-led, parenting course designed to give groups of parents the opportunity to share their experiences, learn from each other and discover some principles of parenting. It is suitable for anyone who is a parent or is planning to become a parent.

The Parentalk Parenting Course features:

Steve Chalke – TV Presenter; author on parenting and family issues; father of four and **Parentalk** Founder.
Rob Parsons – author of *The Sixty Minute Father*; regular TV and radio contributor; and Executive Director of Care for the Family.
Dr Caroline Dickinson – inner city-based GP and specialist in obstetrics, gynaecology and paediatrics.
Kate Robbins – well-known actress and comedienne.

Each **Parentalk** session is packed with group activities and discussion starters.

Made up of eight sessions, the **Parentalk** Parenting Course is easy to use and includes everything you need to host a group of up to ten parents.

Each Parentalk Course Pack contains:
• A **Parentalk** Video
• Extensive, easy to use, group leader's guide
• Ten copies of the full-colour course material for members
• Photocopiable sheets/OHP masters

Price £49.95

Additional participant materials are available so that the course can be run again and again.

To order your copy, or to find out more, please contact:

Paren talk
PO Box 23142, London SE1 0ZT
Tel: 0171 450 9072 *or* 0171 450 9073
Fax: 0171 450 9060
e-mail: pa.rentalk@virgin.net

How to Succeed as a Parent

Steve Chalke

Did you notice when your child was born that the instruction manual was missing?

But help is at hand! Father of four, Steve Chalke, shares some of the many insights his gained during his 15 year struggle with parenthood in this easy to read, practical guide to a hazardous but rewarding task. Full of wise quotations and helpful hints.

- What is a parent's job description?
- How to say sorry for your mistakes
- How to avoid lecturing a 2-year-old or talking down to a 12-year-old
- How to praise, not put down
- How to punish crimes, not mistakes
- How to get the most from your child's education
- How and when to tell your child about the facts of life
- How to let go

Babies don't come with a set of instructions and that's why this positive, no nonsense, funny guide is an absolute must. Every parent should rush out and buy a copy.

Lorraine Kelly, GMTV and Talk Radio Presenter

Published by Hodder and Stoughton
ISBN 0 340 67903 4

The **Paren**talk Guide to the Toddler Years
Steve Chalke

From their first word, their first step, or their first morning in nursery or play-school, being parent to a toddler is exciting, challenging and a great big adventure. But as any toddler's parent knows, it's not always plain sailing – sometimes we wonder how the cute, gurgling, doe-eyed bundle of joy has become transformed, seemingly overnight, into a yelling, iron-willed individual who can turn on a temper tantrum as easily as flicking a switch.

Full of anecdotes, this down to earth guide will provide reassurance and practical tips for parents of toddlers everywhere. Father of four Steve Chalke talks humorously about his own and other parents' experiences and provides invaluable advice for any parent in, or about to enter, this stage of their child's development.

Published by Hodder and Stoughton
ISBN 0 340 72167 7

The **Paren**talk Guide to the Teenage Years
Steve Chalke

Teenagers are a strange breed. They listen to different music to you, wear clothes that seem to be intended to shock you and they even stay up into hours you'd forgotten existed. For many parents the 'onslaught' of the teenage years seems to hit them overnight. It can be rather surprising and frequently daunting.

The Parentalk Guide to the Teenage Years will answer some of your questions as well as offering tips on how to build and maintain a good relationship with your teenager. Other issues covered include knowing how to build a positive self-image in your child's teenage years and also letting go of your child as they enter into their own adult lives. This is an honest and practical book. Full of real-life illustrations, this book will help you on your way to becoming a better parent of your teenagers.

Published by Hodder and Stoughton
ISBN 0 340 72169 3